I HAVE FOUND THE SAVIOR, COME AND SEE

Footsteps of a Jamaican

A book of testimonies

Melbourne C. Powell

Napoca Star

2023

CONTENTS

DEDICATION

This book is dedicated to my Lord and Saviour Jesus Christ, without Him writing this book would not be possible.

Acknowledgments

With God all things are possible.(Matthew 19:26). This was certainly the case in writing this book. All glory is given to God for His inspiration in writing this book. Without God, this would not be possible. I would like to say a big thank you to my sisters Tenza and Trissanne Powell for taking the time to read chapters from my manuscript and giving their feedback.

Thank you very much Christina Boeriu, for reading my manuscript, giving your feedback, and for all your selfless support. "The fact that you have passed through these experiences makes what you are saying more credible." Cristina Boeriu.

Introduction

Have you ever been at the lowest point in your life, that dark place where pain and a feeling of worthlessness reign supreme? I was there. Yes. To that place where living becomes painful and death seems a sweet release. If you have been through struggles in your life then this book is for you. It is well known that loneliness takes over at that low point in our lives, which leads us to believe that life is not worth living anymore. As a result, many turn to substance abuse as a coping mechanism, while some resort to taking medication. Running away from home and substance abuse was my choice of release.

What if there was a simpler solution with lasting results? There is. I have tried and tested it, so with absolute certainty, I know that it works. When we can understand the root cause of our problems, fixing them will become far easier than we think, because all we need to do then is ask the right person for help. I did it. I have friends that did it and even upon writing this introduction, I am helping a friend who is making miraculous progress.

The interesting fact is that I have friends whom I helped to get out of that dark place and I have been to that place. Although we share different experiences and different degrees of hurt and pain, the method of overcoming those difficult times are the same.

It is very imperative if you are at that dark chapter in your life, that you don't think to yourself, nothing can be done or that you are going to wait for a particular time to start making changes. This is very dangerous because the darkness only gets darker if we don't shine The Light into it.

I, like many others, kept saying; I am ok, and everything will be fine. However, things were just getting worse and worse without any rays of sunshine in sight. Holding onto my past was affecting my future far more than I even realized. Looking back with the weight of the world off my shoulders and the bright beams of the sun shining in all the once-dark places of my mind and life, I am filled with unspeakable joy.

I can assure you also that this book will be a great testament to hope. You will be directed to the only true way to peace. Then all those dark clouds will be a thing of the past.

Don't wait to start reading this book, it could be that, in doing so, you will lose valuable time that may not be redeemable. My regret even today is that I didn't come to the knowledge of what is written in this book sooner.

I intend to take you, the reader, on a journey of deliverance, from lost hope to the greatest hope, while carefully laying out the path to true happiness and everlasting life. I found the deliverer, come and see.

Chapter 1

Running The Race Of life

How many times in life have you heard the phrase? "The race is not for the fit or the strong but who can endure to the end." How do you apply this? Do you apply it to your life or a literal race? The scriptures talk about the race of life that we are to endure to the end. "I again saw under the sun that the race is not to the swift and the battle is not to the warriors, and neither is bread to the wise nor wealth to the discerning, nor favor to the skillful; for time and chance overtake them all." (Ecclesiastes 9:11).

We live our lives usually based on how we perceive it, most people based it on their perception of others. But it is when we have the right perspective on life we start to see real changes in our thoughts and actions. The reality is that God is in control of everything. The devil wants us to believe that God has washed His hands off our problems and is no longer interested in the life of sinful men. However, this is a fallacy. The Creator is interested in even the minute details of our lives. We don't need to complicate life with so many definitions of what it is when the Bible makes it so simple and clear.

"For I have taken all this to my heart, even to examine it all, that righteous people, wise people, and their deeds are in the hand of God. People do not know whether it will be love or hatred; anything awaits them. It is the same for all. There is one fate for the righteous and the wicked; for the good, for the clean and the unclean; for the person who offers a sacrifice, and for the one who does not sacrifice. As the good person is, so is the sinner; the one who swears an oath is just like the one who is afraid to swear an oath. This is an evil in everything that is done under the sun, that there is one fate for everyone. Furthermore, the hearts of the sons of mankind are full of evil, and insanity is in their hearts throughout their lives. Afterward, they go to the dead. For whoever is joined to all the living, there is hope; for better a live dog, than a dead lion. For the living know that they will die; but the dead do not know anything, nor do they have a reward any longer, for their memory is forgotten. Indeed their love, their hate, and their zeal have already perished, and they will no longer have a share in all that is done under the sun." (Ecclesiastes 9:1-6).

God has given us the life we have to glorify His name. But because of sin, we have a nature that loves to do evil. As a result, we all share the same fate, which is death. Can we do anything about our fate? By ourselves no, but with God, the one who has everything under control, we can change our fate from death to eternal life. Who doesn't know that one day death will come? Everyone alive knows that they will die. What a wretched and meaningless life it would be if we just live to die. Life would not be worth living. Sadly many people have come to this conclusion, by taking their own life.

A different perspective on life would make such a difference, so much so that the storm of our life would be calmed. As the wise man said under the inspiration of God, better is a live dog, than a dead lion. When we have life we have hope, life allows us to change our perspective and put away all those dark clouds that hide our path. We don't have to carry all our burdens of life, no when we have our burden bearer. "Come unto me, all ye that labor and are heavily laden, and I will give you rest. Take my yoke upon you, and learn of me; for I am meek and lowly in heart: and ye shall find rest unto your souls. For my yoke is easy, and my burden is light." (Matthew 11:28-30). A life with Jesus at the center of it is far easier than one without him. He alone has the real solutions for the problems we face in life.

We are all running the race of life that needs a lot of endurance. However, I have run many endurance races such as; 400m, 800m, 1500m, 3,000m steeplechase, 5000m, and marathons. From those races I came to my first realization of what it means to endure. To be a champion I had to push my body to its limits and stay at that point to the end. But that was not enough, the body can be at its peak of fitness and then you are let down by a weakness of mind. It's like this, if the race is lost mentally, then physically it's lost also. In all the races I won, I was ready mentally, sometimes I was ready more mentally than physically.

At the start of every race, adrenaline is pumping and I feel that I can do this, I will win, this is what I kept telling myself. But during the race when lactic acid starts to build up and the muscles begin to hurt, this is when physical strength is no longer enough. I would have to fight the thought of stopping and learn very quickly to accept the pain and keep going. So many of us have faced indescribable pain and suffering, whether it's due to a tragic loss of a loved one, sickness, trauma, hurt, or separation, it's not a nice place to be mentally or physically. For so many, giving up becomes their only hope. It doesn't have to be this way because God has hope for the hopeless.

When we are going through trials, we focus so much on the problems that we become blind to everything else. Even blind to the fact that in our trials, God is working on us. He allows us to go through these trials, not because He wants us to suffer, no, it's because He knows that it's the only way that we will realize that His way is better. He is not the one that brings us trials, it's our choices and the fact that we live in a world of sin. These facts shouldn't make us feel as if we don't have any hope, because we have great hope in Jesus, "And not only this, but we also celebrate in our tribulations, knowing that tribulation brings about perseverance; and perseverance, proven character; and proven character, hope; and hope does not disappoint, because the love of God has been poured out within our hearts through the Holy Spirit who was given to us." (Romans 5:3-5). We need to exercise faith in what God says in our time of trial, with a clear understanding that God will not break any of His promises to us. He will do whatever He says He will do. Believe His word and do it, He will not fail you.

I had many lessons in life on the importance of having the right perspective but one occasion stood out to me more than the others. I often ask myself, why do we so often choose to run away from our problems? Is it because we are afraid, don't know what to do, want something better or is it just to get away from the pain?

Whatever it is, most of us choose to run away from our problems. Some run to alcoholism, substance abuse, crime, violence, etc. The long-lasting danger is not what we are running from is what we are running to. We can overcome the bad that we are running from only by running to what is good.

At the age of eight, I decided to run away from a bad situation only to end up in another. Living at home became unbearable, my dad was an alcoholic that would go out to drink in the evening and would come home late in the night drunk out of his mind. So much that he would vomit in the one bedroom where we were sleeping. Then he would wake us up and try to beat us for whatever we did wrong days, weeks, or months before. It was a very horrible experience for me and no doubt my other siblings who experienced it. Few years before I witnessed my family being torn apart in a courtroom. The words of the judge printed in my mind. To my mom and dad, he said; "You take the boys and you take the girls." So my brothers and I ended up with my dad and my sisters with my mom. After this, my dad only drank more. What do we run to when we run away?

I decided to run away from home and ended up in a cave up in the hills not very far from my dad's house, where a man called Tony was living. I didn't know much about him because he was a stranger in the area. He is of dark complexion, has natty hair, and seemed to be on the borderline of becoming anorexic. From what I heard he was also running from his problems. I remember him asking me what I am doing up there and I told him that I ran away from home and I am not going back. I remember him saying that my dad will come there looking for me and he will get into problems with my dad for allowing me to stay there. So he decided that we were going to find somewhere else to go. We started to sleep in broken-down houses and bushes, wherever was suitable to stay for the night. We never spent the same night in the same location. Looking back I can see that he saw an opportunity in me, young and naïve. I went with him.

There were warm nights with beautiful stars, nights that were so dark that we walked in thorns without realizing it, we walked on rocky pathways tripping over at times. Rains came and went, our only suit of clothing became wet and dry from body heat, and heavy winds came with their chilling effect as the trees swayed and called out in their ghostly demeanor. On nights I wished for a warm blanket or just an umbrella. Nights I longed to be home, but my home was not a home for me.

We became the Robin Hood of our town, only we were keeping all the spoils for ourselves. We stole food to eat everywhere we went, and most of the time he would send me to go and do it. We spent one entire night breaking into a shop only to get a few cans of milk and nourishment with a packet of biscuits if I remember well. Even falling asleep in the bushes across the road from the shop waiting for it to close, because he had no idea when the closing time was. We were woken up soaked by the rain, he decided to go ahead with his plan anyway. I asked him how he will get into the shop if the door is closed. He said don't worry, just wait here and I will go and check. He was at the side of the shop for what seemed to be forever.

Eventually, he came back and said that he found a way in, he made a hole in the zinc wall and said he will put me through the hole and I should go and open the window for him to come in. So that is what I did and he grabbed all that he could find and said that they didn't leave any money there, let's go. I was so afraid that someone would come and kill us, but he convinced me that the owners of the shop would not hear us because their house was about one hundred meters away from the shop and would be asleep by then. The irony here is that this man was such an unprofessional thief that everywhere he robbed, his victims knew that it was him. He even visited a man's house to ask for marijuana, the man took us to his weed field and said that it was not ready yet. Then that same day at night, he went back and stole many plants from the field.

After robbing the shop and this man's field, he started to travel on roads only at night. During the day we are in the bushes hiding. I don't remember exactly how long I ran away from home but I know that it was for months. That time of sleeping outside aged me so much that I was starting to look less and less like a child even though I was still a child. I spent many nights cold and wet, coughing, and even caught the flu and cold. I thank God that He kept me alive throughout all that experience.

One day Tony went somewhere and came back and said that someone told him that my mom was looking for me. For me, this was very good news, but I was very hesitant to go home because I thought that my dad and my brother were only trying to trick me into coming home. However, Tony said he thinks that it was true, so I should go and check just in case. I believe that it was only by the grace of God, that Tony didn't try to convince me not to go and see. That day was the last day I saw Tony, and many years after my dad told me that the police caught him and he went to prison not long after we parted company. What are we running to when we run away from our problems?

That day I decided to go and see if my mom came to rescue me. I cautiously went towards my house that day hiding in the bushes being careful not to be discovered by anyone. The closer I got to my dad's house the more nervous I became, with my heart pumping out of my chest, because of the fear of getting caught by my dad and eldest brother, it was as if the hand of the Lord was pulling me home. As I struggled with the voice in my head saying; don't go home, you are in so much trouble, your dad will beat you so bad, then another voice said to keep going home. I was now very close to home and I heard the cry of my mother, "Towie my son, come home", it was the cry of someone who it seemed, had lost their loved one. That cry pierced through any doubt I had about going home. I stopped about one hundred meters away to make sure I was hearing correctly because I hadn't heard my mother for such a long time. I could hear my mom cursing my dad and saying how he could let her son run away with a criminal and he is not looking for me.

I heard my dad saying that he sent my big brother to look for me everywhere but he couldn't find me. Well, I didn't want to be found by my dad or my big brother. I sat in the bushes and continued to listen as my mom cried desperately. Wherever you are my son come to me, and I will take you to live with me. Finally, I saw a way of escape. I stood up and walked out of the bushes and went to my mom. I never forgot the look on her face. It was joy mixed with a broken heart. Joy to see me and a broken heart to see the wretched state I was in.

God always has a way of escape for us even in our darkest times. As a heartbroken mother calls her son home, Jesus is calling us home. When we think that no one cares about us. God cares. He cares for all the broken and afflicted souls on this Earth. He cares for me and you. During the time I ran away from home, I didn't think that God was working out a way of escape for me. From my perspective at the time, I was running from problems at home and any situation was better than going home. But the reality is that it wasn't better, but it was the way I took myself out of that situation and God by His grace met me where I was.

I have come to learn that whatever situation we are in, turn to God with earnest prayers and fasting and seek wisdom from Him on how to deal with that particular situation. In doing so we will save ourselves many heartaches and pain.

Chapter 2
Children Obey Your Parents

During my teenage years, I can't say that I was the most obedient child. Although I would like to think that I wasn't the most disobedient. But as the saying goes, a glass of water with a drop of poison is still poisonous. Not being the most disobedient doesn't change the fact that I was disobedient. I remember during the holidays and weekends when my mother had to go to work, she would tell my siblings and me not to leave the house to go to other people's houses or the games field. With her very strong Jamaican accent, she said; "memba mi tell unno, nuh leeve di yaard." But being the disobedient child I was, I just waited until I knew she was on the bus heading to work and then I was off to find all the other teenagers I hung out with.

This urge to go and play with my teenage friends was irresistible. Now you need to understand that summer holidays in Jamaica meant adventure without any parents around to tell me to wash my clothes, sweep the yard, wash the dishes, go get water from the community pipe, or standpipe as it's called in Jamaica and the endless chores that needed to be done.

Summer holidays meant running a boat, which is a Jamaican way of saying we are having a massive cookout, majority of the time I ended up cooking because I was the best at cooking and everyone agreed, so they just find me when it was time to run a boat, going to the river, the beach, playing football and cricket, going to hunt for mangoes and all the best fruits that weren't in my yard. This kind of adventure was never to be missed. Missing the summer adventures with my friends would be like missing the entire year.

So when my mom said not to leave the yard, to me she was saying miss out on all the fun and miss the highlight of the year. Now there wasn't any punishment that was going to stand in the way of a summer holiday to brag about when I get back to school. This is not to rationalize being a disobedient child. No. This is to explain why the urge to go with my friends when they come to call me was irresistible. As a teenager, top on my list of priorities was fun and more fun.

But there was a darker side to my thirsty quest for fun. I wanted to get away from the reality of not having my father around, my mother working hard to support us and send us to school, and a stepdad that had enough of looking after so many children that weren't his. The reality of my impoverished life was pressing me on all sides. At school, I would watch my schoolmates' parents coming to parent meetings and other events where the parents needed to be there. Some would have both parents attending and others one parent or at least a family member, but almost all the time no one came to represent me. Most of the time I had to borrow my friend's mom to represent me.

This is not to say that my mom never came to any of the important events in my life, she did come to a few when she was able to. When she was in Jamaica working, taking time off from work wasn't an option, because that would mean not paying the bills or not being able to go to school. The other times she was abroad working to support us. My mom had to make those sacrifices because my dad was the hands-off kind of dad and my step dad wasn't far behind in this hands-off approach to parenting. Knowing what I know now I understand why they were that way, let's just say that the leaves didn't fall far from their parental tree.

This dark chapter of my life became even darker when I started to be plagued by the supernatural. While growing up in Jamaica I was always confronted with the dark world of black magic, not realizing what it was and the deadly consequences that come with it, even at the age of 6 or 7, I started to ask questions. What is this for? Why do we have bottles buried around the yard? Why do we sprinkle the blood of the chicken around the house when it is killed? Usually, all my questions would be greeted with the answer, "stop asking so many questions, you are too nosy."

My earliest childhood memories at my dad's house consist of me and my brothers and sisters playing hide and seek. I can also remember getting cut on my feet from bottles that were buried in the ground for what seemed many years until they just fell to pieces. However, I could still find bottles buried under trees with liquid inside and it was very clear that they were not for watering the plants, because they were sealed. I remembered asking my eldest brother what they were and he said to leave them as they were for protection. I didn't pursue my line of questioning, because it was clear that he didn't want to explain to me what was going on.

I also remembered that my dad had a collection of fragrant oils with different names, like protection, good luck, safe travels, and so on. If I remember well. What I am sure about here is that my dad used to tip these oils depending on what the occasion was, on his finger then rub them on our forehead and neck. Then he would say that it's to ward off evil spirits. Only if he knew that the spirits he was trying to ward off, by doing what he did, were bringing them to us and himself. It's like leaving your house open for the thief. Many people don't believe black magic is real and I understand, I was one of those people until it was done to me.

After I left my dad's house in the countryside to live close to the city of Kingston. I was looking forward to a better life as promised by my mother. This was because I ran away from my dad's house at about age 8 and ended up pursuing a life of crime with the community thief called Tony. I think I was on the run for a few months while being hunted down by my big brother, who had no idea that I knew where he was, but he couldn't find me. Sometimes I even came into the yard and they didn't know I was there. This brief life of robbing shops and waking up soaking wet and very cold at night taught me many lessons but the one that stuck with me is that we must never follow bad company.

On my arrival in Kingston 9, Saint Andrew after missing many years of school, my mom got me into school at age 8. I was a very poor reader, so much so that when I read something I stuck on most words and sounded as if I was counting very slowly instead of reading. Things were looking up, I left my old life of crime behind at the age of eight, or so it seemed, to pursue a better life. This dream of a better life came to an abrupt end when in the first week of school a bully decided that all the chairs in the classroom were his and I couldn't sit on any of them. What he didn't know was that I have been fighting for survival all eight years of my very short life, well so it seems then. I know who kept me and who was fighting my battles for me. That bully decided that he was going to come and push me after I told him that I will sit wherever I want, then he dared to throw a punch at me. Let's just say that I dodged that punch and landed one straight in his mouth. From that day onwards no one in that school tried to bully me.

In life not every problem can be solved with a punch, I have learned that it's better to take a punch than give one. Because you never know when life will give you back what you give. Here I am not talking about karma. I don't believe in such things. I believe that every wicked person has a day of retribution. We must never wish bad for others, but seek good for everyone. If you have been through very painful life experiences, please don't make things worse by holding on to anger and hatred towards the people who have done you wrong. It is this that destroys your soul and keeps you in the chains of depression. If you truly want to break free then you must forgive, and be reminded that I don't use the word "must forgive" lightly. Without true forgiveness, you will never heal. Because we don't have what it takes in us to forgive, our sinful nature forbids it, we need to look to Jesus' examples and follow them. But first, we must forgive our trespassers, repent of our sins, then go to God to ask for our sins to be forgiven.

It was not long after moving to live with my mom and stepdad, I realized that my past was merging with the then present. The subtle hints of black magic started to become more and more apparent, buried broken and unbroken bottles in the yard and under trees all around the house. When a chicken is killed it was the same as at my dad's house. My stepdad would go and sprinkle the blood around the house. As I got older he would sometimes ask me to go and do it and when I started to become more aware of what was happening, I refused to do it. He wasn't happy but by that time I was in my teenage years, give me how much beating you want, but I am still not going to do it. I started to learn more about black magic or obeah from friends and many times heard my mom telling my stepdad to stop going to obeah man to waste his money and that he should remove all the obeah working bottles he have around the house.

I bet he wishes he had listened when one night about 9 or 10 pm, we heard rumblings in the wildflowers outside and then a loud cry; help! help! Then he ran so fast through the back door into the house, with absolute shock on his face, wet from the sweat running down his face said; "a little girl just slapped me down the gully in the bushes and just disappear in front of me," even now I can't help but laugh uncontrollably about it, then he started to ask if any of us saw the little girl or if it was my youngest sister who did it and ran off into the dark, but it couldn't have been her, because we were all inside the house when it happened. Where we lived was on the side of a hill literally in the bushes about 5-10 minutes from the road and no little girl was going to be there walking around at that time of the night as it's pitch black where there's no light. After that experience, everyone for a while was afraid to go out at night and the outside light at the side of the house where he was slapped, which he neglected to fix, got fixed not long after.

Time passed and that very strong little girl was forgotten. But things started to happen that soon brought back memories of that little girl. The thought of whether my stepdad was telling the truth about the slap in his face by the little girl always lingered in my mind. I heard many things about black magic by this point and just dismissed it as some elderly people's superstitions. How wrong I was.

I can't remember the exact time the dreams came, but I believe it was not long before I started high school at about age 14. First I started dreaming that I was falling from the sky or off a building and I would wake up before I hit the ground with such a frightening feeling that even today I can't explain it. Sometimes I would wake up from the dream and when I went back to sleep, the dream just continued from where it stopped. Every time I had this dream, a feeling of helplessness came over me. It's like being thrown overboard without a life raft and not being able to swim.

However, this was just the beginning. I started to have an experience where I was half awake and trying to get up from the bed, but something was holding me down. I struggled and screamed, but was powerless to do anything. After this heart-wrenching experience, I would jump up from bed screaming my head off from being frightened almost to death. Can you imagine having this same dream almost every night for months? I got to a point where I was afraid to fall asleep.

My nightmares didn't end there, I started having this dream where everything seemed so real as if I was awake and going through the experience. I could feel the beams from the sunrise shining through the window, I could hear talking and even feel the wind blowing. Everything felt real. So the dreams would start in the same order all the time, first I am falling, then held down on the bed, and after the worst of all, hearing the door knock and start to open while I am trying to get up and something is holding me down.

Then I struggle and turn my head to see who was at the door and it was someone without a head or someone with a head and without a body or someone that looks like a shadow that I can see through. This for me was worst than torture and it happened night after night sometimes two to three times in one night. I became terrified of ever falling asleep because as soon as I did it seemed that these nightmares started.

I tried many times to tell anyone I could trust about my dreams, but they would just joke about it and say something like I ate too late or duppy must be haunting me. However, no one took it seriously. I didn't talk about it at school, because I didn't want anyone to make fun of me. So I lived with these nightmares for months upon months without any end in sight. A breath of fresh air came when I went into Mr. Denton's class. As mentioned before, when I moved from the countryside to live with my mom, I was a very poor reader and was struggling to keep up in all my classes.

Then by the providence of God, Mr. Denton was the most peculiar man I have ever met until this point.

He was a disciplinarian and everyone who is in his class must be dressed according to school regulations, be on time always, don't speak during the lesson, and do homework on time. He did what he said and kept his promises, he gave extra lessons free of charge and was a vegetarian. This was the class for the slow kids who needed a push start, I certainly needed a push start.

I remember upon moving to his class, everyone was tested on their reading ability and most of the class was poor readers. The strangest thing for me at the time was that he started to teach us to read from the bible and he was even very sure that we will be reading very well in no time. Well. What is strange about that? He was teaching us to read from the Kings James Bible and for those who don't know it's written in old English. I couldn't understand what I was reading and no one else could. But he said to keep reading. Then after we read a certain amount, he would explain what it meant and I am telling you I was drawn in by the wonderful stories that were in the bible. Within a matter of months if not sooner I noticed that I was not counting my words anymore, but reading very fluently. I saw a miracle happen before my eyes and I got a bible for myself and took it home and put it next to my pillow. I found solace in psalms 51, 27, 124, 127, and 129. Whenever the dream came and I got up and read these scriptures, I would not be harassed again and the dreams went. Many nights I neglected to pray and read my bible and when the nightmares came they were more dreadful than before.

Before the evil spirits with and without heads or the ones with shadows would half open the door and peep around at me, but now they were running towards me and walking through the closed door or just appearing next to me. I would find myself screaming so hard that I would break out into a sweat. I would also wake up screaming my head off from being scared senseless. I couldn't explain or understand what was happening to me or why it was happening, but I was certain that I wanted it to stop immediately. But as I have learned things don't always work out the way you want them, or when you want. All things indeed happen in their time, but in such darkness, I wish I knew the words of the lord that says all things work together for good. I couldn't see it then, but even during these dreadful times of my life God was with me all the way and was leading me to himself. When I look back I realize how many times death came knocking at my door.

The tainted stink of death was to come in its most deceptive and frightening form yet. God gives us warnings of impending dangers and certain death. However, we are more likely than ever to ignore those warnings. If it wasn't for the infinite and persevering love of God, we would all certainly be dead. If there was ever a warning from my mother I must listen, this would be it. I didn't always listen to what my mom said, but I wouldn't let her know that I didn't and if she told me to get something done, I would do it. I just wouldn't stay at home all day and not leave the yard. When it came to playing and having fun, listening to mom's instructions didn't take priority. Time passed and I was still having horrible nightmares, though not as frequent. Then one day I noticed something very strange. It was night and I was alone at home. By this time my mom had moved to England, then my youngest sister and I were waiting to finish school to move there also. So I was living with my step dad and my youngest brother.

Since I started living in my step dad's house, I can't remember one night when he slept somewhere other than his house during the week. Even on weekends when he is not working, he would be back by at least midnight. He was just not the sleeping-out type. He occasionally takes trips to visit his mom and family in another parish for the weekend, but I knew that wasn't the case because I saw him late in the evening and usually when he is going to the country as I have observed many times, most of his family that lives in the community would be going also and it would be such a big excitement that also the entire community would know that there's a trip to the country. My youngest brother would usually be with him, but on this occasion, I noticed I didn't see him with my stepdad that evening.

But this night no such thing happened. All of a sudden he became the person who didn't come home as usual. Because of my dreams, I was also afraid to stay in the house alone at night, and that night was no exception. Midnight passed and I began to wonder if he was coming or maybe he was just running a bit late. It got later and later, while I struggled to keep my eyes open. Fighting to stay awake it was now approaching 3 am if my memory serves me well. Still, he wasn't at home yet. Not being able to fight off my tiredness anymore. I reluctantly fell asleep accepting my faith.

That night my dream started differently than usual, pinning me to the bed in a sick attempt at submission. Everything felt real like never before. I could feel the sun shining just as if I was outside sitting in the sun, I could feel the draft passing over me as if I was awake. Everything felt so much like I was awake that I thought I was. Then I heard a voice saying; do exactly what she tells you. Then my mother appeared before my bed, so radiant as the midday sun, full of unexplainable joy bearing a basket on her head, and as she got closer to me she moved the basket to her hand and sat on the bed next to me.

The basket was full of fruits and vegetables. I can remember pineapple, tomatoes, Thyme, sweet peppers, and spring onions. As my mom sat next to me she said; ever you don't get up to open the door. It was the most direct and stern instruction I ever heard, as soon as she told me that she vanished into thin air right before my eyes. Then the door knocked and the voice of my friend called me to come and open the door. I was about to jump up and open the door as I always did when my friend came to see me. But suddenly the voice of my mom replayed in my mind and now I was the one pinning myself to the bed in obedience to that voice.

I remembered that whenever my friend came to call me, it was time to play football, cricket or run a boat, so I would fly up out of bed as they say in Jamaica. But this time there wasn't going to be any flying up out of the bed. Still, as a sniper, I lay in bed, and the knocking and calling grew louder and more frequent. Then a sudden impatient tone burst into my ears and his voice grew stronger and monstrous. If evil was a voice that would be it. As the voice got deeper the knocking sounded as if someone was breaking down the door.

By this point, I was overwhelmed by the shivers and trills rushing through my body. To say that I was frightened would be an understatement. I don't know how I didn't lose control of my bodily functions. After the final knock on the door that sounded like a bomb went off, I heard and felt such a strong gust of wind pass over my bed and shook the glass panes windows so hard that it woke me up. I noticed that it was dawn as it started to get bright outside. It's good that the day was approaching because, after that experience, I certainly didn't want to sleep anymore.

In Jamaica we have a phrase which I am sure it's not only used in Jamaica that goes like this; I smell a rat. Which is to say that I know that someone is up to no good. I was smelling a rat the night before when my step dad didn't come home as usual, but what happened next made that rat so stink that I found it. After my ordeal the night before, the only place I could turn was to my bible. This was the only place I could find peace. After reading a few scriptures and meditating on what happened.

It was now about 7 or 8 am, when I heard the door opening quietly, then slowly the footsteps moved closer and closer to my room, then my room door was open ajar and the head of my stepdad peeped into the room checking, he never did that before so I stood up and said firmly. Yes! I am still alive. I know you went obeah man to kill me. Then I pointed to my bible next to my pillow and said, a God mi serve and I know what you did. You should have seen the shock on his face, he looked at me as if he had seen a ghost and didn't say a word.

He just left the house. After that day it was like I didn't exist. When he cooked. He would just make food for himself or just cook a lot of what I don't eat. Even in these circumstances, I didn't go hungry, because God provided for me in many ways and fed me like Elijah as I traveled the wilderness of this life. When he finally broke his silence he said that I must leave his house, because he doesn't want me there anymore. I asked him where he wanted me to go and he responded that he doesn't care and I should let my mother find somewhere for me to go.

Many would say that I was lucky to be alive after that night, but I don't believe in luck, because that's for people who don't believe in God. If it was not for the Lord that is on my side, when my enemies rose against me I would stumble and fall. But God Himself spoke through my mom, who is still alive, for evil spirits come in the form of dead loved ones. He saved me from certain death if I had got up from my bed and heeded the call of that evil voice. Only in heaven, I will know what happened that night and I pray that I will make it there by the grace of God. Our eyes are veiled from seeing the spiritual world because our mortal eyes and brains couldn't cope with the chaos and the implications. But one day the veil on the spiritual world will be taken away. Then whatever our beliefs, we all will have to face it.

The word of God opens our minds to the unseen mystery of God and we are given enough information for our salvation. However, in our mortal state, we cannot fathom the depths of the things of God. We often question God and ask; why does He allow all these bad things to happen if he is such a good God? As if to put one's morality higher than the One that created us. God knows the past, present and future and He is not limited by time. He will make all things good, as was originally intended in His own time.

He speaks and it is done and who can undo what He has done? I have learned that without trials in my life, I am as good as dead. When we understand our nature according to the word of God, we realize that we can do nothing, absolutely nothing good without God and we would never make any move to do good without God inspiring us to do so, it is then we see that the trials in our life are like a little nudge in the right direction. Without that little nudge, we wouldn't move. So we should never blame or curse God when we meet difficulties in life, but face them with the assurance that God is refining us like gold in the Refiners' fire.

Time passed and I have been told so many times to leave the house by my stepdad, that now I was sleeping at my friend's house and when I couldn't sleep there, I had to find the most comfortable bush to sleep in. I remember one night sleeping under some trees that looked as if they would keep me dry if it rains. This was close to the main road next to one of our neighbors that everyone called Mr. Palmer. I went to sleep that night in the bushes next to their gate and woke up soaking wet as it was pouring down. I knew then that sleeping outside was not going to be an option and was a reminder of when I ran away from home. This was during the school holidays and I knew that I had to find somewhere to live before school reopens. I continued bouncing from house to house and bush to bush until I had to go back to my stepdad.

When he came home and saw me there he was mad, he said didn't I tell you mi no want you a mi yard? Dogs are treated better, I couldn't help but feel like that. I told him that I was not leaving until my mother said to leave. To say this to him came from God, because it was my stepdad who was communicating with my mom and updating her on what was happening, and after I said that he stopped asking me to leave. Eventually, I managed to get a calling card to call my mother and told her that my step dad wanted me to leave his house.

She said that he didn't tell her that when he was asking her to send money for me . After this, all hell broke loose. One day he was very angry and he came home saying that my mother went foreign and she is not coming back, so leave my house or he will kick me out. I said no; I am not going anywhere. He went under the bed in his bedroom with his machete and came to me saying to me leave his house before he has to kill me. I ran into the kitchen for a knife as it was the only close weapon I could find. I guess at 15 years of age, I was yet to grasp that a knife has no business in a machete fight.

We were now standing close to the doorway between my room and his room. He continued shouting, come out of my house before I have to kill you. I said to him that if he even comes near me with the machete I will stab him. He ran up to me and took such a big fast swing that I didn't even see it coming. However, what happened next can only be explained as God's intervention. Even though I didn't see the machete coming at me, I fell back so fast as if I was pulled out of the way. Just enough so that I could feel the wind of the tip of the machete as it passed my neck and lodged inside the doorpost.

The swing he took at me was so powerful that he couldn't remove the machete from the doorpost. Then I heard one voice say to stab him now and another said don't kill him. So I gave him just a little prick from the knife. I was thinking that I must show him that I will not let him kill me if he manages to remove the machete. I gave him the small cut on his belly and he ran out of the house and was gone for some time. After she came with his sons and brother all adults and came with cussing and death threats after death threats. That day I left the house and went to my neighbor and told them what happened. They told me not to go back there and she contacted my mom and told her what happened. My mom made arrangements with her for me to stay there until she was able to sort out the paperwork for me to come to live with her in England.

The next day I was sitting on the main road at the big house gate where most of the people in the community, young and old usually hang out. As I sat talking with my friends a police jeep came and stopped in front of us. Two policemen came out with M16 in hand and called me to come to them with hands up and asked if it was me who tried to kill my stepdad. I said to them that It was him who tried to kill me and I was defending myself.

They said to explain everything that happened and I did, then they asked me what my mother and father's names were, and when

I told them they quickly got in the jeep and said stay out of trouble and left. Sometime after this school was reopened and my school break from hell was over thankfully. I came home from school one evening and I heard that a man who looked just like me was there that day. It so happened that I ran into my dad in the town that evening on the way from school and we talked for some time. His line of questioning was definitely to find out if I was ok and what was happening with me and my stepdad. I explained to him and he assured me that he sorted the problem out. Since I left my dad's house he never came to see us in the city, but after my stepdad did what he did, he came to the community. I don't know what he did there that day, but after that, my step dad walked on the other side of the road when he saw me.

Looking back I can see the hand of God taking care of me and preventing the hand of death from falling on me. I know that if God would remove His protection from us for only a second, Satan, the devil would wipe us off the face of the earth. But our Lord and Savior Jesus Christ loves and cares for every one of us individually as if we were the only one on earth. What can separate us from the love of God?

It's very important if you have been through similar circumstances in your life to forgive, holding on to unforgiveness will cause far more damage than the experience itself. True forgiveness means taking all the hurt and pain and laying it at the feet of Jesus and moving on with your life, not allowing your past to affect your future. It also means letting that person who hurt you know that you have forgiven them. Believe me when I tell you that absolutely no medicine is better than forgiveness in this kind of situation. When God heals us He deals with the root cause of our sickness, so that it doesn't come back as a problem in our lives. Many years after this experience I went to Jamaica and thanks to God that He put in me to go and visit my step dad and assist him how I could. The light that shines through us comes from Jesus Christ, the same love and mercy that He extends to us must be extended to others regardless of who they are. Are we not all Sinners in need of a Saviour?

Chapter 3

How I found the truth

Many people spend their life searching for the truth or the meaning of life itself but end up never finding it. It is not as simple as doing a google search or looking it up in the dictionary. No, it's far more complicated than that for many, and yet so very simple. From the perspective of worldly wisdom truth is defined as being relative, according to Wikipedia; Relativism is a family of philosophical views which deny claims to objectivity within a particular domain and assert that facts in that domain are relative to the perspective of an observer or the context in which they are assessed. There are many different forms of relativism, with a great deal of variation in scope and differing degrees of controversy among them.

In layman's terms this is saying that there are many truths and those truths are defined as truth in the context of the individual's assessment of it. The reality of what they are saying here is that two individuals can read the same statement of fact and then make up their own truth about it, because the focus is on how the statement is perceived and not whether it's factual or not.

In an article on motherjones.com titled; A conversation with Robert Thurman, we can gauge how one of the world's most respected religious figures views truth.

Thurman: You speak about how the Buddha always emphasized the rational pursuit of truth. "He instructed his disciples to critically judge his words before accepting them. He always advocated reason over blind faith." Coming from a late 20th-century belief that there is no Truth, only contingent truths, how are we to imagine what the Buddha meant by "truth" in contemporary terms?

Dalai Lama: Buddha was speaking about reality. Reality may be one, in its deepest essence, but Buddha also stated that all propositions about reality are only contingent. Reality is devoid of any intrinsic identity that can be captured by any one single proposition — that is what Buddha meant by "voidness." Therefore, Buddhism strongly discourages blind faith and fanaticism.

Of course, there are different truths on different levels. Things are true relative to other things; "long" and "short" relate to each other, "high" and "low," and so on. But is there any absolute truth? Something self-sufficient, independently true in itself? I don't think so.

In Buddhism, we have the concept of "interpretable truths," teachings that are reasonable and logical for certain people in certain situations. Buddha himself taught different teachings to different people under different circumstances. For some people, there are beliefs based on a Creator. For others, no Creator. The only "definitive truth" for Buddhism is the absolute negation of any one truth as the Definitive Truth.

Thurman: Isn't that because it is dangerous for one religion to consider it as the only truth?

Dalai Lama: Yes. I always say there should be pluralism — the concept of many religions, many truths. But we must also be careful not to become nihilistic.

From this conversation, it's safe to conclude that the Dalai Lama doesn't believe that there's a Definitive or Absolute Truth. He considers it dangerous for any religion to consider itself to have the only truth. He is a proponent of pluralism. He is not alone in his pluralistic view as many people globally share the same view. However, if experience is anything to go by, the majority is not always right.

The martyrs of the dark ages who accepted the Bible as the word of God and absolute truth, were hunted down like animals and killed. If history is to teach us anything, it should be never to trust the kind of thinking that leads us to believe that there is more than one truth. I know the dangers of groups or individuals believing that they are right and everyone else is wrong. In the past, this has led to tyranny and the loss of millions of lives. There are elements of truth in every religion. However, elements of truth are not absolute truths. The great art of deception is to combine truth with lies. Satan has perfected this art. Isn't it logical that truth is truth and everything that is not truth must then be a lie? Which leads me to argue that if the creator of the universe is the God of truth, why would He not also be the proponent of absolute truth?

We can spend eternity, if we had that long, arguing that there are many truths and end up at the same point. If there are many truths, we can also conclude that there's no lie, because what lies in someone else's reality might be the truth in mine, according to their rational, and that's a lie within itself. Every religion can't be the truth if it has an element of a lie in it. One might ask, well then, how do we know which one is telling the truth? Well, human beings have been redefining the truth ever since the dawn of sin and the only thing that has changed is the name given to it, pluralism, relativism, many truths, our truth, my truth, etc. It is all just fancy ways of saying, I am a liar. All lies originate from the father of lies, just as all truth originates from the Father of truth. Many may say that they don't agree with what I am saying, because they are not religious, and that's ok, but that doesn't change the fact that there's truth and there's a lie and none of them agrees with each other. Pretty much like religion isn't it? To find truth you must find the origin of truth.

NASA spends billions of dollars to find the origin of the universe when they could get the answer for free. To think that they will spend even more and never find the truth, if they continue to look in the wrong place. A well-known preacher in his sermon once said; "they could give him one red penny and he would tell them." Then he quoted Genesis 1:1 which says; "In the beginning, God created heaven and the earth." For many people, the obvious truth is not so obvious. It's like being told, "you are what you eat" and then we eat things that are bad for us with the expectation of good health. So how does all of what is said, lead anyone to the truth? Well, what is the truth? The Bible tells us that a historical figure called Pontius Pilate, governor of Rome during the time of Jesus Christ asked that very same question. Maybe he was just being "jesting pilate" as he is often referred to, but what was ironic is that the origin of truth was standing before him. Not being able to recognize truth, like many, his perception of truth has been debased due to constant rejection of what is obvious.

Therefore Pilate said to Him, "So You are a king?" Jesus answered, "You say correctly that I am a king. For this, I have been born, and for this I have come into the world, to testify to the truth. Everyone who is of the truth hears My voice." Pilate said to Him, "What is truth?" And after saying this, he came out again to the Jews and said to them, "I find no grounds at all for charges in His case. (John 18:37-38 N). If anyone wishes to become part of the truth, then they should listen to the voice of truth. Notice that the text didn't say a truth, it uses the definite article "the" to show us that the text is referring to something specific, something previously mentioned or known, something unique, or something being identified by the speaker. In John 14:6 Jesus saith unto him; "I am the way, the truth, and the life: no man cometh unto the Father, but by me." We can see that man's ideas of relativism and pluralism are far away from God's ideal. 1 John 5:20 says; "And we know that the Son of God has come, and hath given us an understanding, that we may know him that is true, and we are in him that is true, even in his Son Jesus Christ. This is the true God, and eternal life."

So how do we know for sure that the God who says that He is the truth is the real deal? It so happens that He has set a challenge for all the other so-called gods to come and prove themselves. Exodus 15:11-13 says; "Who is like You among the gods, Lord? Who is like You, majestic in holiness, Awesome in praises, working wonders? You reached out with Your right hand, The earth swallowed them. In Your faithfulness You have led the people whom You have redeemed; In Your strength, You have guided them to Your holy habitation." Isaiah 40:25-26 says; "To whom then will ye liken me, or shall I be equal? saith the Holy One. Lift your eyes on high, and behold who hath created these things, that bringeth out their host by number: he calleth them all by names by the greatness of his might, for that he is strong in power; not one faileth."

The true God of the entire universe claims both Creation and Redemption as His special identifying mark and makes it very clear that no one else is like Him or can be compared to Him. Can anyone else but the true God create life? Can anyone else but the true God redeem us? Pluralism will have its mount Carmel experience and all the prophets of Baal will be exposed. All who have set themselves against the true God of heaven by making themselves enemies of the truth are setting themselves up for failure.

Now that you can grasp where I am at in my thinking, I hope that you have been paying attention, let's go back to see how I got here. My experience with religion started at about age eight when my Aunt dragged me and my younger siblings to Sunday church, the only thing that remains in my mind is the very loud drums, rolling on the floor, lots of babbling, and the preacher shouting down the mic or megaphone throughout the entire visit. Then after church the sweets, cakes, and snacks that both young and old looked forward to. My interest in what was at church stopped at the pastries. How was I to know at that age what the bible teaches if it was not studied even by church members? A great emphasis was placed on music, dance, and display. It was an atmosphere that shocked the senses and drowned out the voice of God. John 2:16 says; "And to those who were selling the doves He said, Take these things away from here; stop making My Father's house a place of business!" Some may interpret what I am saying here as judging, but who am I to judge? I am a sinner like anyone else. If anything, a bigger one. I am merely pointing out the facts.

We can all have solace in the word of God that says; "And the times of this ignorance God winked at; but now commandeth all men everywhere to repent: Because he hath appointed a day, in the which he will judge the world in righteousness by that man whom he hath ordained; whereof he hath given assurance unto all men, in that he hath raised him from the dead." (Acts 17:30-31). God doesn't hold us accountable for what we didn't know, that is not to say that we didn't sin, thus He calls us to repent when we come to the knowledge of the truth. I didn't like going to that church and thank God that my Aunt didn't take us every week and eventually not at all.

My next encounter with religion, many will say that it's a movement and not a religion, is with my dad. He said that he had Rasta in his heart, but he doesn't lax his hair, so he kept it Afro instead. He also painted his house in Rastafarian colors, he tried the ital vegetarian diet at some point in his journey, but didn't maintain it. He also had badges and buttons with Haile Selassie, Former Emperor of Ethiopia. According to Britannica.com; "As emperor of Ethiopia (1930–74), Haile Selassie I was known for modernizing his country, for helping to establish the Organisation of African Unity (now the African Union) in 1963, for his exile (1936–41), and for being overthrown in 1974. He was also regarded as the messiah of the African race by many Rastas. I never got into this religion as I didn't find the truth there. By this stage, I was already reading the Bible and I already knew that there was no mention of Selassie in it. Now I am certain that there isn't even one mention after many years of studying the bible. I am also with a clear understanding that he most definitely doesn't hold the title of creator and redeemer, which makes him fallible like every other human being.

I continued reading the Bible throughout my troubled teenage years, although many of my high school friends thought I had the best life, my life at home proved to be quite the opposite. With all that was happening in my life, I needed strength not to end up on the street or in some gangs or like so many I knew, and substance abuse. Reading the Bible opened up a new world to me, one that I could escape, one that seemed out of this world, in the sense that the stories were absolutely amazing and real, and had so much real impact on my life. When I was sad or wanted to give up on life, I would just open the Bible and the page I opened would have just the words of strength, compassion, and care that I needed. How God works in our life is mind-boggling, the depth in which He cares for us is extraordinary, for an infinite God to place so much care on even the finite things in my life, proves to me that He is like no other.

The more I read the Bible I started to realize that many of the things I heard about God from most religions were not true. Like being burned in hell forever. As popular as this teaching is, it is an error on the highest level. Just as Satan misquoted scripture in the garden of Eden, he has been doing the same throughout the ages, even today deceiving many. However, we don't have to allow ourselves to be deceived, especially when God has given us all the light we need in His word. We just need to search for that light and He will reveal it to us. I searched for that light, because the God that was working in my life and carrying me throughout my difficult times, didn't seem to be the same God that would leave people to burn in hell forever. It just didn't make any sense to me. After studying the scriptures that speak about the wicked being sent to hell to be burnt in everlasting fire. It became clear what the deception was. "Then shall he say also unto them on the left hand, Depart from me, ye cursed, into everlasting fire, prepared for the devil and his angels:" (Matthew 25:41). "And these shall go away into everlasting punishment: but the righteous into life eternal." (Matthew 25:46).

A surface reading of these Bible verses would now conclude that the wicked will be cast into eternal fire. The trouble here is that God did not call us to be surface readers. The Bible tells us that we are to compare scriptures with scriptures. "For precept must be upon precept, precept upon precept; line upon line, line upon line; here a little, and there a little: For with stammering lips and another tongue will he speak to these people. To whom he said, this is the rest wherewith ye may cause the weary to rest; and this is the refreshing: yet they would not hear. But the word of the Lord was unto them precept upon precept, precept upon precept; line upon line, line upon line; here a little, and there a little; that they might go, and fall backward, and be broken, and snared, and taken." (Isaiah 28:10-13). Here we can see God directing us to study His word with due diligence.

"But the Day of the Lord will come as a thief in the night, in which the heavens shall pass away with a great noise, and the elements shall melt with fervent heat. The earth also and the works that are therein shall be burned up." (2 PETER 3:10). "And when the thousand years are expired, Satan shall be loosed out of his prison, And shall go out to deceive the nations which are in the four quarters of the earth, Gog, and Magog, to gather them together to battle: the number of whom is as the sand of the sea. And they went up on the breadth of the earth and compassed the camp of the saints about, and the beloved city: and fire came down from God out of heaven and devoured them. And the devil that deceived them was cast into the lake of fire and brimstone, where the beast and the false prophet are, and shall be tormented day and night forever and ever. And I saw a great white throne, and him that sat on it, from whose face the earth and the heaven fled away; and there was found no place for them.

And I saw the dead, small and great, stand before God, and the books were opened: and another book was opened, which is the book of life: and the dead were judged out of those things which were written in the books, according to their works. And the sea gave up the dead which was in it, and death and hell delivered up the dead which was in them: and they were judged by every man according to their works. And death and hell were cast into the lake of fire. This is the second death. And whosoever was not found written in the book of life was cast into the lake of fire." (Revelation 20:7-15). "For, behold, the day cometh, that shall burn as an oven; and all the proud, yea, and all that do wickedly, shall be stubble: and the day that cometh shall burn them up, saith the Lord of hosts, that it shall leave them neither root nor branch. But unto you, that fear my name shall the Sun of righteousness arise with healing in his wings, and ye shall go forth, and grow up as calves of the stall. And ye shall tread down the wicked; for they shall be ashes under the soles of your feet on the day that I shall do this, saith the Lord of hosts." (Malachi 4:1-3).

As we can see clearly from the scriptures hell doesn't exist yet, one obvious clue is that the earth is not melting from fervent heat. We can also see that the earth is where Satan along with his angels and all the wicked will be destroyed. We see that the wicked will be burnt to ashes. There is no eternal burning in hell if the wicked are burnt to ashes. So what happens after the wicked and burnt up? God creates a new heaven and a new earth. "For, behold, I create new heavens and a new earth: and the former shall not be remembered, nor come into mind." (Isaiah 65:17). "And I saw a new heaven and a new earth: for the first heaven and the first earth were passed away, and there was no more sea." (Revelation 21:1).

When I came to this understanding my view of God changed, He was no longer this vindictive sadist as the world portrays Him. I knew that He cared even about the little things in my life and now, I was starting to see He is not just sitting in heaven waiting for me to sin so that He can put me in hell. No. Certainly not. God is now working on our behalf, with desperation to save every sin-sick soul. He would rather empty all of the resources of heaven to come to the aid of one lost soul. God truly loves us.

"For God so loved the world, that he gave him only begotten Son, that whosoever believeth in him should not perish, but have everlasting life." (John 3:16).

The correct understanding of who God was gave me so much strength that whatever trials came in my life, I knew that God will take care of them if I just ask Him to do it. Accepting the truth by the grace of God became easy, and simply because I tried Him at His word and saw that His word was good. He said that He would deliver if I asked according to His will and he has been delivering me throughout many hard times. After I came to the understanding that I have access to an infinite God with infinite power, my problems became finite.

When I went to high school I started to do religious education. I remember being taught the many different gods that are revered in so many religions of the world. The more I learned about them the more I started to realize that the God that was so involved in my life could not be compared to them. To me these gods never checked to see how I am doing, they don't inquire about the small details of my life. They don't feed me when I am hungry and they don't look after me when I run away from home. All I could see in the depictions or writings about those gods was chaos. Half man and half animal, inanimate objects, greed, pride, and fleshly lust, were the main characteristics of these idols. As someone who was searching for the truth, I didn't see the truth in these religions. Some had elements of truth, but for me, that was just not enough. I wanted to know the full and absolute truth.

During my primary years, I saw nuggets of that truth being practiced by my school teacher. I noticed that he was patient and well disciplined, very polite and respectful. He was determined that all his students should be the best, not just in their studies but in character also. He would even do extra classes for free to help the weaker students get up to scratch. I was one of those weaker students, a very poor reader, I was able to read as if I was counting, hardly able to pronounce big words or read a full sentence. However, I remember him saying that I will get you to read properly in a very short time. He gave me a Bible to take home and read, also our reading lessons at school would be from the Bible. The stories that were being read from the Bible in these classes, caught my attention as nothing has before. It was as if my mind was finally opened and all the clutter was removed. Within a term, if I remember well, I became a very confident reader. Today I still tell others that the Bible taught me how to read.

The character of my teacher was different from the other teachers and I saw that it came from Bible principles. I knew this because he usually said, do you know that God said that you should behave this way and that way when he is correcting our bad behaviors? More and more I started to see the defects of my character because the Bible stories we were reading opened them to me brighter. Still, I didn't understand what I needed to do, because by this point the churches I was going, didn't teach me anything other than to avoid going to those churches that I went to. Why? The music was deafening, people jumped and shouted, lots of babbling, and a lack of Bible teachings. I could find no peace in such places and so I wanted to avoid them.

It was not until I was in high school that God's providence came in the form of a friend, who invited me to come to her baptism and I went. At this point, I didn't know much about baptism and why anyone ever needed to do it. Only that you do it to wash off the devil. If that was the case, when we decide to get baptized we might as well stay in the baptismal pool. Satan doesn't quit in his fight against us, so as soon as we leave the pool we would need to get back in again to wash him off. These misconceptions were about to change as I sat to witness her baptism.

However, the first thing that caught my attention was not the baptism itself. It was the actual atmosphere in the church. The calmness and peace that was in this church must have been how it felt when Jesus calmed the stormy seas as His disciples were panic-stricken. I could feel the stormy seas of my life being calmed as I sat there and listened to hymns that had not blessed my ears before. For the first time, I was in a church where there was no bedlam or noises. There was no "getting into the spirit" , a babbling of confusion. Then it was the baptismal service itself. I could see that it was a solemn occasion. From that day I realized two things. I realized that I needed to get baptized and what church I should get baptized into.

I believe that God blesses us richly when we do things with the right motives. Deep inside our hearts we always have a reason why we do something and with our fallen nature and the Spirit of Christ void in our lives, our motives usually take on a selfish nature. Our love of self can only be rooted out by our love of Christ our savior.

"Let this mind be in you, which was also in Christ Jesus: Who, being in the form of God, thought it not robbery to be equal with God: But made himself of no reputation, and took upon him the form of a servant, and was made in the likeness of men: And being found in fashion as a man, he humbled himself, and became obedient unto death, even the death of the cross. Wherefore God also hath highly exalted him, and given him a name which is above every name: That at the name of Jesus, every knee should bow, of things in heaven, and things in earth, and things under the earth; And that every tongue should confess that Jesus Christ is Lord, to the glory of God the Father." (Philippians 2:5-11).

Our Lord and Saviour Jesus Christ have given us many lessons on unselfishness. However, the one that stands out to me the most is the fact that the King of the universe, the Creator of everything created, the Alpha and Omega, would humble Himself to such a level as becoming like one of His creations. I was thinking about what earthly analogy to use in comparing such selflessness, but could not find any, because no one else had what Jesus had and gave it up. Not for Himself but for us and to vindicate His father's name. Such a selfless act just can't be compared. "It is not the greatness of the work, but the love with which it is done, the motive underlying the action, that determines its worth." (5T 279.2).

"God is represented as weighing all men, their words, their deeds, their motives, that which determines character. "The Lord is a God of knowledge, and by Him, actions are weighed." "Men of low degree are vanity, and men of high degree are a lie: to be laid in the balance, they are altogether lighter than vanity." "Thou, most upright, dost weigh the path of the just." "All the ways of a man are clean in his own eyes, but the Lord weigheth the spirits." Important lessons are suggested to us in these scriptures. There is not a thought or motive in the heart that God is not acquainted with. He sees all as clearly as if it stood out registered in living characters, and He weighs individual motives and actions." (TM 438.2).

I don't profess to know the motives of anyone, I can't even work out my motives, because of my deceitful heart. Not wanting to fool myself into believing that I know my motives for doing good or evil, I asked God to give me a heart like His, so that His motives can be mine also. "If the Lord searches the heart, I try the reins, even to give every man according to his ways, and according to the fruit of his doings." (Jeremiah 17:10). The Lord is the one who knows who we truly are. He knows what is in our deepest thoughts and understands clearly the reason for our every action.

"He knows what is in our hearts and what we are thinking." (John 2:24; Matthew 9:4). The mind and the heart are interconnected, in-fact they are one of the same. "For as he thinketh in his heart, so is he: Eat and drink, saith he to thee; but his heart is not with thee." (Proverbs 23:7). It is where the character is formed and developed.

What was in my thoughts when I decided to get baptized for the first time? When I turned 18 years of age and now living in a shared house, somewhere in west London, I became friends with one of the tenants living at the house as well. She presented herself as being very kind and was in many ways, as our friendship grew, I became more and more infatuated with her, even though she was dating someone at the time. She was older than me and by our conversations a lot more experienced in life. I can't remember if I told her that I liked her more than just friends or if she picked up on it. However, the conversation came up one day and I told her. She then said to me that she knew someone more beautiful than her, my age and she would be a lot better for me to have a relationship with. I asked her who this person was and she said that it was her sister and she was coming to live in England a few months from that day. I was intrigued and very excited. If ever there was a case that raging teenage hormones make us irrational in our thinking and actions, this would be it.

"More beautiful than her" were the words that ruled my thoughts as I anxiously waited to meet this girl. I waited for what seemed forever, only about 3 months if I might add, that one day I met her walking down the stairs of the shared house and she didn't disappoint. She was very beautiful and straight away my infatuation took over and suddenly I was in love with her. I know all of us have been there at some point in our lives believing that we truly love someone when we know absolutely nothing about them. We may think that we love someone we didn't take the time to know, but it's the outward appearance and the thought of what we believe that the person can offer us we are truly in love with. The reality is that we are in love with the idea of who we think the person is and not the actual person.

We started dating about 4 or 5 months before she told me that she is going home. At that time it was devastating news for me, I started to get over my infatuation the more I got to know her, and now she was leaving. What? Why?! I thought you were here to live. What is going on? It's like giving me my favorite slice of cake and then taking it out of my hand just as I am about to take a bite. It's like having a bucket of July mangoes in front of you and as soon as you take one up to sink your teeth in it, you wake up and realize that it's just a dream. Well, you get the point. It was not good news for me.

I started to ask her about all that was happening and she told me that her visa was only for six months. She applied for an extension and they rejected it. By this time I was already in the army and was in a position to help her by getting married. The only thing was that I wasn't even thinking about marriage. I was young and wanted to wait until I had my own house and car first. But there I was, 18 years old and caught between a rock and a hard place. The thought came to my mind of whether to cut my losses or help her, I was thinking about it until about a month before she had to leave the country if I remember well. In the end, I felt that the right thing to do was to help her. I could not help but feel roped into marriage from the very beginning, but this was the start of my first baptismal journey.

So how did I decide to get baptized the first time? My girlfriend at that time's parents were Seventh-day Adventists and would not approve of our marriage without both of us getting baptized. So we decided to get baptized together before we got married. However, the pastor of our local church would not baptize me because I was still in military service and would not be able to keep the Sabbath. I am not sure who came up with the idea but she told me that there was going to be an evangelism camp meeting soon, somewhere in London, and after it, we can get baptized. All I can remember of that event was that we were waiting awhile for our names to be called to go inside the baptismal pool. We got baptized together and became members of a Seventh-Day Adventist church in the London Borough of Ealing. While the wedding was being planned we attended that church and started Bible study about our beliefs. Most of the planning for the wedding was done by her because I was in army cadet training.

Looking back it is clear to me that my motive for getting baptized was so that I could marry her. However, that motive is questionable, because I wasn't even thinking of getting married until I got my own house and car. The truth is that I wanted to get to know her without worrying about any marriage yet. To get baptized for such a selfish reason wasn't based on a conviction of heart but rather selfishness. Starting any kind of relationship like that is doomed for failure. After baptism not much changed in our lives, we were just going to church but there was no change to the life we were living before. We went further away from God. Many of us base baptism on our feelings, I was one, believing that as soon as I come up out of the water I will feel less of a sinner and my life will just miraculously get better, I will feel saved. Thank God that salvation is not based on our feelings, that would be a travesty at the uttermost. As much as I was expecting to feel different after baptism, I didn't feel any different contrary to my misconceptions. I was very ignorant about what baptism means.

However, God is wisdom and He gives it to all who come to Him seeking it. What is baptism? "Therefore we are buried with Him by baptism into death: that like Christ was raised from the dead by the glory of the Father, even so, we also should walk in the newness of life." (Romans 6: 4). Christ has made baptism the sign of entrance to His spiritual kingdom…He has made this a positive condition with which all must comply with who wish to be acknowledged as under the authority of the Father, the Son, and the Holy Spirit. . . .

Baptism is a most solemn renunciation of the world. (Testimonies, vol. 6, 91:2, 3). I was still sadly living a worldly life with failures and disappointments as a norm.

It was Jesus himself who commanded His disciples to go to all the world and baptize others, teaching them all what He taught them. "Go ye therefore, and teach all nations, baptizing them in the name of the Father, and the Son, and the Holy Ghost: Teaching them to observe all things whatsoever I have commanded you: and, lo, I am with you always, even unto the end of the world. Amen." (Matthew 28:19-20). "Know ye not, that so many of us who were baptized into Jesus Christ were baptized into his death? Therefore we are buried with him by baptism into death: that like Christ was raised from the dead by the glory of the Father, even so, we also should walk in the newness of life." (Romans 6:3-4).

Baptism is a public renunciation of our old life as it is performed in front of the members of the church you are getting baptized in. As the individual is submerged this symbolizes the acceptance of Christ's death on the cross for our sins and dying to a life of sin. As we ascend out of the watery grave, this symbolizes our rise to a new life. A life that despises all sinful words, thoughts, and actions. Notice that there is no mention of feelings here, the focus is on Jesus and our walk with Him. This solemn act of baptism is a memorial of His death, burial and resurrection.

The more I learned about baptism, the more I realized how unprepared I was to get baptized when I did it the first time. I thought I knew what I was doing but I didn't. Could I have known more? Certainly. With more study and preparation. Before baptism, we are to be instructed in the teachings of Jesus. The Ethiopian eunuch was studying the teaching of Jesus through the writings of Isaiah the prophet and when he came to the true understanding of the gospel of Christ, he was ready to be baptized.

In Paul's ministry, we can see many re-baptized after coming to a better understanding of the teaching of Jesus. "He said unto them, Have ye received the Holy Ghost since ye believed? And they said unto him, We have not so much as heard whether there be any Holy Ghost. And he said unto them, Unto what then were ye baptized? And they said, Unto John's baptism. Then said Paul, John verily baptized with the baptism of repentance, saying unto the people, that they should believe on him which should come after him, that is, on Christ Jesus. When they heard this, they were baptized in the name of the Lord Jesus." (Acts 19:2-5). Jesus himself at the age of 12 as he walked into the temple for the first time came to the full understanding of what His earthly mission was although He got baptized at 30 years of age, according to Jewish custom about the age at which a male can enter the priesthood.

The problem with unpreparedness is that the time needed to get to know Jesus is not spent, it's the same in any marriage relationship. To know someone we must spend quality time with that person. Just learn first how to become good friends. Neither in marriage nor my first baptism did I follow these words of wisdom, and it's because of that I can write from experience. Don't rush into anything. Before we can be truly convicted of our sins, we need to get to know Christ which we have crucified by our sins.

We can't get to know Him and believe Him without learning of Him through His words. This can only be done by spending time studying it. After we come to know Christ the Holy Spirit can do His work of convicting the heart of sin. Then we can truly repent because only now do we see the sinfulness of our sins. Now true repentance can lead to baptism. "Then Peter said unto them, Repent, and be baptized every one of you in the name of Jesus Christ for the remission of sins, and ye shall receive the gift of the

Holy Ghost." (Acts 2:38). Now that we have believed, repented, and baptized the Holy Ghost floods our hearts with inexpressible joy, peace, and happiness. He shines a light through your soul in such a way that you can't stop talking about Jesus the one who rescued you. Now the taste of old life is no more. We walk daily living a new life in Christ Jesus.

The popular teaching of modern Christianity today doesn't reflect the biblical teaching on baptism. All the spiritual and symbolic meaning is sprinkled away by the flick of a wrist or by the shake of a hand. However, in scripture baptism by immersion can only be found. "John also was baptized in Aenon near Salim, because there was much water there." (John 3: 23). "Jesus, when He was baptized, went up straightway out of the water." (Matthew 3:16). "They went down both into the water, both Philip and the eunuch; and he baptized him." (Acts 8: 38). "And when they came up out of the water." (Acts 8:39). There is overwhelming evidence in regards to the kind of baptism the Bible recognizes as the true baptism, and if that wasn't clear enough God went even further so we may understand clearly. "One Lord, one faith, one baptism." (Ephesians 4:5). "Those who are baptized in the threefold name of the Father, the Son, and the Holy Spirit, at the very entrance of their Christian life declare publicly that they have forsaken the service of Satan and have become members of the royal family, children of the heavenly King." (Testimonies, vol. 6, 91:3).

I didn't come to the true understanding of what it means to get baptized until my second time, after thirteen of the most miserable years of my life. After leaving the church because I wrongly thought that it was the right thing to do after being let down more than once by a church leader who promised to come and counsel us during the failure of my marriage. I would like to make it very clear that once you have decided to give your heart to Jesus and become a member of His church, there should never be any reason for you to get up and leave. The moment we go into a church and start looking at the other sin-sick souls there as our example, we are setting ourselves up for failure. Jesus should be our only example, and when He is, we become an example for others.

After thirteen years of waywardness, I was at the lowest point in my life. I was so far gone from Jesus that I didn't even remember that there was a Seventh-Day Adventist church. It was now about 2014 and my marriage to the "more beautiful than me" lady had ended bitterly after about eighteen months. As far as I am aware, we have forgiven each other and are now brothers and sisters in Christ. My life away from the church was filled with alcohol, women, marijuana, and parties. I have no doubt that my lifestyle at the time contributed to the marriage breakdown. All of which are destructive to everything a person can be. I was clubbing so much that at one point I was going there every night from Thursday-Sunday, until after many years, one night I was standing in a club in Bedford, Bedfordshire England, when a voice spoke to me in my mind, clear as day. "What are you doing here?"

That voice lingered in my thoughts for many other club nights as an overwhelming thought among the numbness of an intoxicated mind full of profane music and the licentiousness of the club environment. Until one night I asked myself out loud, what am I doing here? For years I have been going to the club wasting my money listening to the same kind of music week after week. Just wasting my life away. Not long after I left the club by the grace of God never to return. The following year I was in church preparing for baptism and after I completed the course, I was baptized for the second time. God is not limited in His ability to save us. His light can shine even to the deepest depths of the darkness of our hearts and if we listen to the knocking of His wonderful voice on the doors of our hearts, surrender to Him, then He will save us even to the uttermost.

Chapter 5

Bible Study

I have to confess that for many years I was surface reading the Bible. Throughout my teenage years and into adult life, I would occasionally read just a few chapters in the book of Psalms and a few verses here and there throughout the Bible. Until my adult years after getting baptized, I haven't as much as read a quarter of the Bible much less studied it. Some people have also read the Bible more than once but never actually studied it. No wonder so many people are puzzled why Christians read the same Bible, but still, there are so many different denominations. It was not until I started to study specific doctrines of the Bible such as; the sanctuary, the state of the dead, the Sabbath, the spirit of prophecy, and the second coming of Jesus Christ, that I came to the realization of how little I knew of what the Bible taught.

Isn't that the case for the majority of professing Christians today? We do not take enough time to dig deep enough into God's word to find the hidden treasure. We are often overwhelmed by a world of cares, trying to get through our daily lives, paying the rent or mortgage, sending our children to school, trying to get a good education, or just scraping through life by the skin of our teeth. Whichever way we choose to get through life, whether by working very hard or just idling our way to the grave, we are giving one life to live and what we do with it has eternal consequences.

When I first started to seek God through His word, I didn't know where to go or who to ask as I wasn't going to church yet. So like many, I went to YouTube and did a search on the Sabbath and found a well known Jewish individual from America teaching about the feast days and the Sabbath. The more I watched his teachings the more confused I became, why? He was talking about the sign of the red heifer and the prophecy being fulfilled. He also spoke a lot about the rebuilding of the temple in Jerusalem and the coming Messiah.

It wasn't long before I started to realize that he wasn't talking about the second coming of Jesus, but instead the first. I didn't know much about the bible but I knew this much that the Messiah already came. That was one of the reasons I started to have my doubts about his teachings, then it was the heifer and the feasts days in regards to them being reinstated. All that was enough for me to widen my search about the Sabbath.

I watched many other videos talking about the sabbath until I started to realize that the most popular videos were teaching about the Jewish Sabbath, then the Sunday Sabbath, and somewhere down the search list is the biblical Sabbath. In other words, if we are looking at popular videos to learn about the Biblical Sabbath, we would not learn about it.

After I realized that I was only learning false gospels, I started to rethink the way that I was seeking to study the bible. Usually, I would just take up the bible and read it but, I wasn't making the many connections to be made. I knew nothing about comparing scriptures with scriptures.

I got to the point where God led me to Seventh-day Adventist videos teaching about the Sabbath. However, I didn't know how to study the bible until I came across William Miller's writings on how to study the bible. He did this step-by-step guide showing from scripture, what the bible says about studying it. I believe that the best person to tell us how to study the bible is the One who inspired it.

I heard a long time ago from someone that the acronym for the word Bible means basic instructions before leaving earth. I often wonder what those basic instructions were, but never took the time to find out. I just kept telling myself that I will do it later or tomorrow. The reality is that for many, that time never comes. The Spirit of God is constantly working on our hearts, to soften them so that we can hear the voice of God. The more we reject that call to righteousness the more difficult it becomes for us to answer it.

As soon as we enter the education systems of the world that reject the principles of Christ's teachings, we find ourselves in a situation where we are taught to believe that the universe came about just by chance, that all the well-taught laws of nature and nature itself are just coincidental. It's like saying that the bees just know it should take pollen from one flower to another and just by coincidence pollination occurs and the plant produces food for humans and animals.

But at the same time, we are told by the same earthly wise men, that if all the bees died, eventually all life would die. Why not say that by chance all life would survive if all the bees die?

Because by chance everything would just evolve its way out of any such a crisis. The argument is that we came to live by chance, so if we all died by chance, we should be able to live again by chance. How ridiculous. Some have bought into the idea that these intricate, and also fragile details of nature's development occured over millions of years of evolution. The problem with this idea is that neither the Bible nor nature gives a record of such a theory. A careful study of nature, void of such deception, will always lead the mind to the word of God.

The Creator of heaven and the earth and all things that are in them, Jesus Christ, has not left us without an abundance of evidence in nature to prove what is said in scripture and of His existence, so that we may believe and repent. However, we often allow the media and our social circle to influence our understanding of who God truly is. The danger in this is that we will never get to know God truly, without carefully studying His word and living it. "The fear of the Lord is the beginning of wisdom: and the knowledge of the holy is understanding." Proverbs 9:10. The word fear in the text quoted above does not imply that we are to be afraid of God, although that is the image that the devil has painted of God throughout the ages. Rather it's about obedience to God, showing reverence to Him simply because He is our Creator.

"Let us hear the conclusion of the whole matter: Fear God, and keep his commandments: for this is the whole duty of man. For God shall bring every work into judgment, with every secret thing, whether it be good, or whether it be evil." Ecclesiastes (12:13-14).

We can see clearly that to fear God means obeying His commandments. Careful looking at Proverbs 9:10, I can also see that true wisdom starts with obeying God and a knowledge of Him gives us understanding. So many people use the very short time that we are given on this earth, when compared to eternity, trying to find out the meaning of life and where we came from when the answer is already given and is irrefutable by the abundance of evidence in scripture and nature.

"What? know ye not that your body is the temple of the Holy Ghost which is in you, which ye have of God, and ye are not your own?

For ye are bought with a price: therefore glorify God in your body, and in your spirit, which is God's." (1 Corinthians 6:19-20). When we put away all preconceived ideas of who God is and study the Bible, all of life's small and great questions are answered, most of the time God answers these questions so simply, that it baffles the worldly wise men and in other cases, so profound that we are not able to understand it yet. But the fact remains that God has given us the answers for all that we need to know to prepare us for eternal life and they can be found in His word.

After I gave my life to Jesus and started to study the Bible, I saw a change taking place. Firstly, I noticed that I was looking back on my life more than ever, not to glory in how I have lived, instead, it was looking at how I have lived it. It was very clear to me that, the more time I spent getting to know Jesus through the scriptures, the more I started to see how much of a wretched man I was. Secondly, I started to see the man I put on the cross and continue to put Him there, whenever I chose to sin. He was not just any man in my eyes, because now I knew that He was the same person who formed our first parents Adam and Eve with His own hands and breathed the breath of life into their nostrils and they became living souls. When they fell into sin, Jesus was the one who asked His Father to take the punishment for sin on our behalf.

He was the same person who saved the human race from total self-annihilation, by a flood sent by God in the time of Noah, because the sins of humanity got so great that all of the people at that time were about to be overrun by the assails of Satan. But God saw faith in Noah and his family and only eight were saved from the flood. He was the same person who parted the Red Sea to deliver His people from the bondage of slavery in Egypt. He gave the Ten Commandments on Sinai and renewed His covenant with His people. Then I behold that same Man, the Almighty God, our Creator, nailed to the cross, bearing the sins of humanity. Then I saw that it was me who caused the shedding of such innocent blood, by my life of sin. Yet He died for me and us all. That by His death we may have life and have it abundantly.

The Bible doesn't lie, I was coming to understand from studying scripture and receiving the knowledge of God. Not only of who God is, but who I am and who I can become. My life, all the ups and downs, and all the things happening in the world started to make sense. I now have a new insight into the great controversy between good and evil that started in heaven. When Satan the adversary started to war against God's government. Satan, a created being, wanted things to be done his way, instead of the way of the one who created him. I could see now that my life had a better purpose than I originally thought. Life wasn't just about making money and having a family, as good as those things are, they don't address the problem of sin that is in me.

I started to realize that God had called me to a life of service, He is calling everyone, but not everyone chose to answer, to share His word with others but most importantly to be different from the world, to live a righteous life. Am I there yet? No. Will I get there? God said that with Him I can and I believe Him. Lord, please help me to become a true steward of your heavenly kingdom. Amen. When God calls us, it's to a life of sacrifice, so many are reluctant to answer, but when I consider that Jesus made the greatest sacrifice for us and He did it voluntarily, I think that whatever sacrifice I need to make is minuscule in comparison.

The more I learned about Jesus the more I wanted to share what I knew with others. I did it so much that I started to realize that He was all I wanted to talk to anyone about. As much as it's good to want to talk about Jesus, from my experience it's better to speak about Him when asked about Him and constantly live like Him. Do not make the same mistakes I did as a baby in the faith, I was called a Bible basher a few times and was avoided many times because I was only focusing on the theory of Jesus when people wanted to see Him in practice. I realized that I was a better witness to God when I started to find out what the needs of the people in my sphere of influence were and meet them. It is well known that Jesus won many souls and did little preaching. This is not to say that preaching is not necessary, it is a very important part of witnessing. But as Christ has shown, action speaks louder.

I started to see that the word of God had the power to change my life and the relationship I had with others. No longer was I holding on to unforgiveness and by the grace of God I was able to put away my pride and apologize to the people who I have done wrong and to those who have done me wrong. If you are reading this and I have done you wrong and didn't apologize, I am truly sorry, please forgive me and feel free to speak to me about it, maybe I have no idea that I did you wrong. I have learned that in the fight against good and evil, we are all sinners and all in need of forgiveness. It makes absolutely no sense to focus on the bad others have done to us, instead, we are to understand that we are in a spiritual warfare that requires spiritual weapons. Keeping our minds on evil thoughts produces evil actions. The best way to overcome evil is with love, the same love that Jesus Christ has shown us, while we were yet sinners, He sacrificed Himself for us by dying for our sins on Calvary's cross.

From studying the word of God I have come to the understanding that no one was born into this world to satisfy worldly requirements. We are not here just to live and die. We were born on this earth to glorify God and in doing so, God says to all His people who obey His voice so clearly spoken in scripture, "But ye are a chosen generation, a royal priesthood, a holy nation, a peculiar people; that ye should shew forth the praises of him who hath called you out of darkness into his marvelous light; Which in time past were not a people, but are now the people of God: which had not obtained mercy, but now have obtained mercy." (1 Peter 2:9-10).

The mercy that God extended to us by sending His own Son to die for our sins, should never be kept to ourselves. Many are waiting for that hand of mercy to be extended to them, so Jesus said to us to let the light in us that came from Him shines to others.

When I got baptized and started to do even more Bible study. I had the overwhelming feeling to share what I learned with others. I wasn't sure what my talent was, until God opened my eyes, to see that people are usually very open with me when it comes to asking me for advice. Most times we would end up speaking for hours looking at ways to resolve whatever problems they had.

Looking back it's ironic that I couldn't find anyone to help me resolve my problems. I think it's because everyone I knew had something to resolve. Isn't that how we all are in a world marred by sin? The enemy is always attacking us, Satan doesn't let go of us so easily when we choose to follow Jesus. "Yet Michael the archangel, when contending with the devil he disputed about the body of Moses, durst not bring against him a railing accusation, but said, The Lord rebuke thee." (Jude 9). The devil claims us as his own and will not let us go without a fight.

I was shown in my transformation experience with God when He spoke to me that love is the answer to what I was searching for and to what He wanted me to do. This love was not according to the worldly understanding of love. The world associates love with possession, so we tend to believe that if someone doesn't give us material things then it's not love. I love myself, my car, my house, my good job, my clothes, and so on, are usually the way the majority of us view love. Worldly love is materialistic in its foundation and stems from the pride of Satan.

This was not the kind of love that God wanted me to understand. So He told me to first go to my family and friends who I had any disagreements with, even if I think that I wasn't at fault, and apologize to them. I started to contact everyone I could. This experience was very eye-opening for me, because I realized that all the grudges that I held inside of me for so long, were part of my life's burdens until that point. I saw how my friends and families have been swept away, that I could even apologize for what I did wrong, much more to apologize for what they did by taking the blame on myself.

I didn't realize the power of forgiveness and love until I saw what going to my families and friends in humility did to them and myself. It gives healing to the soul. If we all choose to make peace with God and others we would cast out the dark clouds of depression that clouds our mind.

I started to see that true love is not expecting someone to do something for you or give you something all the time. It was what you gave. It is worth understanding here that of ourselves we have only hate, pain, and all manner of evil to give. We are all sinners. God needs to put His love in our hearts, so that we can have love to give. This love is one in which we stop being selfish and become selfless. What greater expression of love can we give than to sacrifice ourselves for others? "For God so loved the world, that he gave him only begotten Son, that whosoever believeth in him should not perish, but have everlasting life." (John 3:16).

Both God the Father and His Son Jesus Christ, have shown us by their actions, that true love is about giving and sacrificing ourselves for others even when they did nothing to deserve it. This is the very essence of true evangelism. Everyone who has truly beheld the uplifted Saviour and understands that it is our sins that crucified Him, their hearts will break into pieces knowing that they did such a thing to someone who truly loves them.

This is exactly what the Gospel teaches everyone who will hear it. The devil knows this, so instead, he filled us with pride and unforgiveness which becomes a barrier to true love in our lives. Many times I have fallen under this deception, trying to convince people how much of the Bible I knew, without true love for them in my heart. We have to allow God to show us in our ministry, that it's not what we know, it's what we know and do.

There is nothing wrong with knowing the scriptures God said that we should study them, the problem is not doing what we know, which makes us bad witnesses for Jesus. I have shamefully been a bad witness many times in my Christian journey. I pray to God for His forgiveness and His strength to become a good witness.

The work of evangelism is a very grave matter as it pertains to the issue of life or death. Every disciple of Jesus Christ is a steward of the heavenly kingdom. We are here on earth plagued by sin and must work together with Christ to seek and save the lost. "Go ye therefore, and teach all nations, baptizing them in the name of the Father, and the Son, and the Holy Ghost: Teaching them to observe all things whatsoever I have commanded you: and, lo, I am with you always, even unto the end of the world. Amen. (Matthew 28:19-20).

I saw the necessity of the messengers, especially, watching and checking all fanaticism wherever they might see it rise. Satan is pressing in on every side, and unless we watch for him, have our eyes open to his devices and snares, and have on the whole armor of God, the fiery darts of the wicked will hit us. There are many precious truths contained in the Word of God, but it is the "present truth" that the flock needs now. I have seen the danger of the messengers running off from the important points of present truth, to dwell upon subjects that are not calculated to unite the flock and sanctify the soul. Satan will here take every possible advantage to injure the cause. (EW 63.1).

But such subjects as the sanctuary, in connection with the 2300 days, the commandments of God, and the faith of Jesus, are perfectly calculated to explain the past Advent movement and show what our present position is, establish the faith of the doubting, and give certainty to the glorious future. These, I have frequently seen, were the principal subjects on which the messengers should dwell. (EW 63.2).

Speaking the truth is not always welcome by everyone, it is a fact that the majority will reject it. This doesn't mean that we should give up on someone, because they reject the message we are preaching. Preach the word and leave the Holy Spirit of God to do the work of convicting the soul. God is long-suffering and we should be also. I have seen rejection in my ministry while preaching present truth, biblical doctrine for the time in which we live, doctrines such as the sanctuary, the investigative judgment, and the health messages met bitter resistance. So much that I almost got disfellowshipped, but by the grace of God, a church vote prevented it.

This should not deter any of God's servants, persecution is to be expected when we teach and preach the undiluted Gospel of Jesus Christ. The millions of martyrs are a testament to this fact. If we hold firmly onto Jesus and keep our eyes focused on Him, then whatever happens we can have faith that He will deliver His faithful ones. "But watch thou in all things, endure afflictions, do the work of an evangelist, make full proof of thy ministry." (2 Timothy 4:5).

God will always be faithful to all who are faithful to Him. We may fall off the path occasionally, but our spiritual journey should always be heading upward to Jesus. Our character is seen by our works, not by the good or bad we do occasionally, but by a consistent life speaking and doing the will of God. Everyone will show who they serve by what they did will all God has given them. Our talents, ability and intellect are all taken into consideration when our life comes before the judgment seat of God.

Chapter 7

Two Marriages

Most often we attribute the breakdown of marriages to these major categories; Financial problems, infidelity, lack of communication, and abuse. There is no doubt that these problems destroy marriages. I have seen these factors causing the breakdown of my marriage.

I have seen many relationships that seem to be going well ended, and when asked what happened, usually the answer is, he or she is useless, they can't look after me, I want better, I want to travel like my friends and family are doing, I want a better house, I want a better car, etc.

The interesting thing about the fairytale love that has been sold to us from the dawn of sin has selfishness in its core principles. It teaches that we should go into a relationship to receive only and not to contribute anything. We are cursed with this selfish nature, that leads us to believe that a marriage can only be good when we are on the receiving side, but if there ever comes a point when we have to give, or even worst give and get nothing in return, all of hell breaks loose and Mr or Mrs love is thrown out the window.

This fairytale idea of a true marriage can be seen in the media. This false depiction of marriage removes selflessness, sacrifice, true love, and faithfulness. This can also be seen in the amount of marriage between people with wealth that carries a prenuptial agreement.

This just underlines our materialistic approach to marriage and in general, the majority of us may not have the wealth to make a prenup, but we make our conditions on who to marry based more on financial and materialistic things rather than looks per se. Not that a marriage based on looks has any more chance of serving.

When we take our marriage vow, we promise to be with each other through the good and bad times. But the strength of our promises is always tested when the hard times come around. Why are we so quick to divorce when things don't work out the way we wanted them to? It's very easy for us to point our finger at the other person and blame them, that they are the reason the marriage is not working or has ended. It's very unusual for us to take the blame also and acknowledge our role.

Most of us are driven by pride and will not allow our other half to know the real reason we decided to get married to them. Finding out this will cause our perfectly painted image to be marred. So we keep our pride and continue with our theatrical performance, picking at every little thing and finding fault where there's no fault. Eventually, we get to the point where nothing the person we professed our love to does is ever good enough.

Then from small arguments to bitter enemies and in some cases sadly. Death. Many will argue that if a marriage consists of good communication, good finances, faithfulness, and trust, then that marriage will most certainly continue until death. However, I disagree because many marriages fit these criteria and still fall apart.

Because of this, I believe that we need to look deeper than what is the visible cause of the breakdown of marriages. We need to understand that our physical problems have spiritual roots. For example, we are naturally selfish because we have an inherent selfish nature. To become unselfish requires getting rid of our selfish nature. The problem here is that we can't overcome our spiritual defects by ourselves. We need someone outside of ourselves with the power to do it.

The root cause of marriage breakdown and divorce is our relationship with God. The issues such as lack of communication, unfaithfulness, finances, and abuse are the effects of not having a good relationship with God.

I once heard a story told of an alcoholic husband, who would go out and get drunk with his friends and then take them home late in the night and wake up his wife to make them food. The wife was one that never complained as she was a Christian woman who loved God and understood that the real enemy was not her husband although it was very easy to make him the enemy.

She knew that she was up against principalities and powers in high places. "Put on the whole armor of God, that ye may be able to stand against the wiles of the devil. For we wrestle not against flesh and blood, but against principalities, against powers, against the rulers of the darkness of this world, against spiritual wickedness in high places." (Ephesians 6:11-12). If that woman decided to fight with her husband to be heard or get things the way she wanted them to be, she would lose that fight. However, when we allow God to fight our battles not even the devil can win against us.

God alone can shine His light into the darkness of our hearts, and root out the selfishness and pride that holds us captive. When Peter told Jesus that it was beneath Him to die for the salvation of mankind, He spoke to the person that was influencing the words coming out of Peter's mouth. "Get thee behind me satan." Peter, like many others, was looking for a great king that would start a revolution and overthrow the Roman yoke of bondage that they were under.

How many of us enter into marriages expecting to live the same life we were living as a single person? Believing that marriage should be without commitment, and when it is required by the individual receiving a lack of commitment, the one who is not committed, starts to blame the other for telling them what to do. This leads the individual to feel undervalued and unappreciated.

The unwillingness to be committed may arise in some cases from past relationships where there was unfaithfulness and abuse that have not been overcome. In this case, committing to another person may seem to the abused individual as if they are given up the freedom they now have after leaving such a relationship. This can also be learned behaviors developed from the traumatic experience of growing up in a broken home or one where the mother or father is not around most of the time.

Then some women hold onto their feminist values, which in turn cause them to detest any idea of subjecting themselves to any patriarchal authority. Anyone with such a mindset should not waste their time and others getting married.

Some may understand that I am saying here that, there are no marriages and no marital relationships, where real cases of compulsive controlling behaviors are present. Not so, I am not ignorant of the fact that this is present in every relationship to varying degrees. Some people are more manipulative than others and are willing to keep doing it for as long as they are allowed to get away with it.

Our Heavenly Father must be looking with broken heart and dismay at how Satan has managed to degrade the holy institution of marriage. Through his deceptions, he has tricked the world into believing that marriage is just words on a piece of paper that has no meaning or long-lasting value.

The Creator Himself, Jesus Christ instituted marriage during the week of creation, which makes it a creation institution. Adam described his wife as being; "bone of his bone and flesh of his flesh." Have we taken any time to consider the deep closeness described in these words? Can we understand the oneness that God requires in a marriage relationship? When we do, we will understand that selfishness is the first spiritual killer in any marriage relationship.

Guess what? We are all naturally selfish. Should we then believe that all marriages are doomed to failure, because of our nature? Certainly not! Our selfish nature can be overcome, by the grace of God along with educating ourselves with God's true ideals for marriages. We also need to put His instructions into practice, because knowing what is right is not enough.

God intended marriage to be sacred between a man and a woman. The boundaries of God's original plan for marriage were crossed millennia ago when Eve invited a fourth party, the serpent, into her marriage relationship. Now we are at a point where the definition of what constitutes a marriage is, so marred all the way to utter confusion and the highest level of licentiousness.

The marriage relationship was intended to teach us about the unity and love that can be found in the Godhead. The Father, The Son, and The Holy Spirit share this unique bond with true love at its foundation. Here you will find absolutely no selfishness, because all members of the Godhead are cooperating and doing everything in the interest of each other and their creation.

In this relationship, there's no fight for power or first place, because everyone puts each other first while respecting each other's responsibilities, roles, and authority. If such a relationship is the practice in earthly marriages, there would never be even one divorce. We may believe that such a marriage is not possible, because this is what we have been led to believe, all marriages have their challenges, and yes, we still live in a sinful world. However, God never tells us to do something without giving us the power to do it.

We are all invited to take part in a marriage that has eternal consequences. If we are to be accepted into that marriage, we must learn and practice the lessons God has given us in our early marriages. We can not treat this marriage as meaningless words on a piece of paper.

"And Jesus answered and spoke unto them again by parables, and said, The kingdom of heaven is like unto a certain king, which made a marriage for his son And sent forth his servants to call them that were bidden to the wedding: and they would not come. Again, he sent forth other servants, saying, Tell them which are bidden, Behold, I have prepared my dinner: my oxen and my fatlings are killed, and all things are ready: come unto the marriage. But they made light of it, and went their ways, one to his farm, another to his merchandise: And the remnant took his servants, and entreated them spitefully, and slew them.

But when the king heard thereof, he was wroth: and he sent forth his armies, and destroyed those murderers, and burned up their city. Then saith he to his servants, The wedding is ready, but they which were bidden were not worthy. Go ye therefore into the highways, and as many as ye shall find, bid to the marriage. So those servants went out into the highways, and gathered together all as many as they found, both bad and good: and the wedding was furnished with guests.

And when the king came in to see the guests, he saw there a man which had not on a wedding garment: And he saith unto him, Friend, how camest thou in hither not having a wedding garment? And he was speechless. Then said the king to the servants, Bind him hand and foot, and take him away, and cast him into outer darkness, there shall be weeping and gnashing of teeth. For many are called, but few are chosen." (Matthew 22:1-14).

"The parable of the wedding garment opens before us a lesson of the highest consequence. The marriage represents the union of humanity with divinity; the wedding garment represents the character which all must possess who shall be accounted fit guests for the wedding." (COL 307.1).

"In this parable, as in that of the great supper, are illustrated the gospel invitation, its rejection by the Jewish people, and the call of mercy to the Gentiles." (COL 307.2).

In the first gospel invitation to the wedding Matthew 22:1-3. The King represents God the father, the Son represents Jesus and the servants represent His messengers. The first messengers came in the form of John the Baptist, the 12 Apostles, and the 70 disciples. "In those days came John the Baptist, preaching in the wilderness of Judaea, And saying, Repent ye: for the kingdom of heaven is at hand." (Matthew 3:1-2).

Then The 12 Apostles were chosen. "These twelve Jesus sent forth, and commanded them, saying, Go not into the way of the Gentiles, and into any city of the Samaritans enter ye not: But go rather to the lost sheep of the house of Israel. And as ye go, preach, saying, "The kingdom of heaven is at hand." (Matthew 10:5-7).

Jesus then appointed 70 disciples. "After these things, the Lord appointed another seventy also, and sent them two and two before his face into every city and place, whether he would come." (Luke 10:1).

The second gospel invitation to the wedding came when the 7 deacons were sent, and His servants; prophets, wise men, and scribes were sent also. "Again, he sent forth other servants, saying,

Tell them which are bidden, Behold, I have prepared my dinner: my oxen and my fatlings are killed, and all things are ready: come unto the marriage. But they made light of it, and went their ways, one to his farm, another to his merchandise: And the remnant took his servants, and entreated them spitefully, and slew them." (Matthew 22:4-7). The sacrifice here represents the death of Jesus. "And in those days, when the number of the disciples was multiplied, there arose a murmuring of the Grecians against the Hebrews, because their widows were neglected in the daily ministration. Then the twelve called the multitude of the disciples unto them, and said, It is not reason that we should leave the word of God, and serve tables. Wherefore, brethren, look ye out among you seven men of honest report, full of the Holy Ghost and wisdom, whom we may appoint over this business." (Acts 6:1-3).

His servants were killed. "Wherefore, behold, I send unto you prophets, and wise men, and scribes: and some of them ye shall kill and crucify; and some of them shall ye scourge in your synagogues, and persecute them from city to city: That upon you may come all the righteous blood shed upon the earth, from the blood of righteous Abel unto the blood of Zacharias son of Barachias, whom ye slew between the temple and the altar. Verily I say unto you, All these things shall come upon this generation." (Matthew 23:34-36). "And they stoned Stephen, calling upon God, and saying, Lord Jesus, receive my spirit. And he kneeled down, and cried with a loud voice, Lord, lay not this sin to their charge. And when he said this, he fell asleep." (Acts 7:59-60).

Peter and John were arrested. "And they laid hands on them, and put them in hold unto the next day: for it was now eventide." (Acts 4:3). Christians were persecuted by Saul. "And Saul was consenting unto his death. And at that time there was a great persecution against the church which was at Jerusalem; and they were all scattered abroad throughout the regions of Judaea and Samaria, except the apostles. And devout men carried Stephen to his burial and made great lamentation over him. As for Saul, he made havoc on the church, entering into every house, and haling men and women committed them to prison." (Acts 8:1-3). "Many both men and women were thrust into prison, and some of the Lord's messengers, as Stephen and James, were put to death." (COL 308.2). Jerusalem was destroyed in AD 70.

The third gospel invitation to the wedding is found in Matthew 22:8-14. "The third call to the feast represents the giving of the gospel to the Gentiles. The king said, "The wedding is ready, but they which were bidden were not worthy. Go ye therefore into the highways, and as many as ye shall find, bid to the marriage." (COL 309.1). Peter takes the gospel to Cornelius. "Then Peter went down to the men which were sent unto him from Cornelius; and said, Behold, I am he whom ye seek: what is the cause wherefore ye have come? And they said, Cornelius the centurion, a just man, and one that feareth God, and of good report among all the nation of the Jews, was warned from God by a holy angel to send for thee into his house, and to hear words of thee." (Acts 10:21-22).

Paul took the gospel to the Gentiles. "As they ministered to the Lord, and fasted, the Holy Ghost said, Separate me Barnabas and Saul for the work whereunto I have called them." (Acts 13:2). "Nevertheless, brethren, I have written the more boldly unto you in some sort, as putting you in mind, because of the grace that is given to me of God, That I should be the minister of Jesus Christ to the Gentiles, ministering the gospel of God, that the offering up of the Gentiles might be acceptable, being sanctified by the Holy Ghost." (Romans 15:15-16).

"In both parables, the feast is provided with guests, but the second shows that there is a preparation to be made by all who attend the feast. Those who neglect this preparation are cast out. "The king came in to see the guests," and "saw there a man which had not on a wedding garment; and he saith unto him, Friend, how camest thou in hither not having a wedding garment? And he was speechless. Then said the king to the servants, Bind him hand and foot, and take him away, and cast him into outer darkness; there shall be weeping and gnashing of teeth." (COL 308.1).

"The call to the feast had been given by Christ's disciples. Our Lord had sent out the twelve and afterward the seventy, proclaiming that the kingdom of God was at hand, and calling upon men to repent and believe the gospel. But the call was not heeded. Those who are bidden to the feast did not come. The servants were sent out later to say, "Behold, I have prepared my dinner; my oxen and my fatlings are killed, and all things are ready: come unto the marriage." This was the message borne to the Jewish nation after the crucifixion of Christ; but the nation that claimed to be God's peculiar people rejected the gospel brought to them in the power of the Holy Spirit. Many did this most scornfully. Others were so exasperated by the offer of salvation, the offer of pardon for rejecting the Lord of glory, that they turned upon the bearers of the message." (COL 308.2).

The third call of the gospel feast has been going on for 2000 years. What garment will we be found wearing? "By the king's examination of the guests at the feast is represented a work of judgment. The guests at the gospel feast are those who profess to serve God, those whose names are written in the book of life. But not all who profess to be Christians are true disciples. Before the final reward is given, it must be decided who is fitted to share the inheritance of the righteous. This decision must be made before the second coming of Christ in the clouds of heaven; for when He comes, His reward is with Him, "to give every man according as his work shall be." (Revelation 22:12).

Before He comes, then, the character of every man's work will have been determined, and to every one of Christ's followers the reward will have been apportioned according to his deeds." (COL 309.3-COL 310.1).

"The wedding garment in the parable represents the pure, spotless character that Christ's true followers will possess. To the church, it is given "that she should be arranged in fine linen, clean and white," "not having spot, or wrinkle, or any such thing." (Revelation 19:8; Ephesians 5:27). The fine linen, says the Scripture, "is the righteousness of saints." (Revelation 19:8). It is the righteousness of Christ, His unblemished character, that through faith is imparted to all who receive Him as their personal Savior." (COL 310.3).

Eternal life is not based on a profession, true is the same for marriage. We need to have the right character, the character of Jesus Christ, and be guided by His Spirit. Without this, we will make our marriage all about us, and in turn, make the life of our spouse a living hell. All things are possible with Jesus Christ, so let us live our marriage on earth as if we were in heaven.

We are doing a great injustice to ourselves when we fail to live our earthly marriages according to God's prescription for marriage. We are missing out on tasting a piece of heaven with our spouse here on earth. The beauty of getting an insight into the closeness of the Godhead, how their selflessness brings inexpressible joy, the results of true unity and a taste of true love. All of which God intended for us as an object lesson of the closeness and love He desires for us to share with Him.

Chapter 8

Diet And The Mind

I have heard the phrase on numerous occasions; "you are what you eat" but never gave it too much consideration. Growing up in Jamaica I never gave too much attention to what I was eating or drinking, sometimes I didn't have a proper meal to eat, so whatever I got was much appreciated. However, growing up in rural areas was a great plus, because living with my dad meant, about ninety percent of what we ate was from his garden. So we knew exactly what we were eating, unlike today with all the pesticides rich and GMOs produced on the market.

Most people, when they think of diet, relate it to going on some strict regime that dictates what they can and can't eat or drink, and in most cases it usually is. However, what we put on, and inside our bodies and in our minds are also part of our diet. So in a sense; we are what we eat, drink, think, and use. For example, we all know that alcohol and drugs are bad for our bodies, but often never consider things such as toiletries and cosmetics as harmful, even though the majority of them contain ingredients that are harmful to our bodies.

What about entertainment? Do we consider movies, music, and arts as containing things that are harmful to our minds? I remembered the first time my primary school had a movie day, after the martial arts film, most of the kids were flying kick off walls, and some into each other, pretending to be the actors in the film. Most parents view movies, music, and arts, as harmless fun, maybe because of ignorance or denial, whatever it is, the bible is very clear; "But we all, with open face beholding as in a glass the glory of the Lord, are changed into the same image from glory to glory, even as by the Spirit of the Lord." (2 Corinthians 3:18). The more time we spend with Jesus through the study of His word, prayer, and ministry, the more we become like Him over time.

Moses while spending time upon the mount with Jesus had to veil his face in front of the people, as the glory of Christ imputed to him was brighter than what the people could behold. Moses became changed by Who he was observing. Does it make any difference whether or not we are beholding good or evil? No. We are changed by what we behold regardless of its nature. The mind when processing information doesn't differentiate between fiction and reality, to the mind information is just information. Without the laws of God, that information will seem to us as harmless.

When I started smoking and drinking, I did everything to hide what I was doing from my mother, because I knew what I was doing was not good and it would disappoint her. However, those convictions weren't enough to stop me from doing it. I came up with many rationales as to why I needed to do it. I kept telling myself that I needed to relax, it is good for my stress, and it's not as bad as people make it out to be. And when the paranoias kicked in from the high levels of THC in my system, I was convinced that everything that was in my mind was reality. My mind became a world where evil is good and good is evil. The reality in which the devil wants us all to live. Society on hold is this reality. In any case, our diet greatly affects our appreciation of the truth.

"You need clear, energetic minds, to appreciate the exalted character of the truth, to value the atonement, and to place the right estimate upon eternal things. If you pursue a wrong course, indulge in wrong habits of eating, and thereby weaken your intellectual powers, you will not place that high estimate upon salvation and eternal life which will inspire you to conform your life to the life of Christ; you will not make those earnest, self-sacrificing efforts for entire conformity to the will of God, which His word requires and which are necessary to give you a moral fitness for the finishing touch of immortality." (Testimonies for the Church 2:66, 1868. CD 47-CD 47.1).

The Bible tells us that God had an ideal diet for us that was given at creation, even before sin entered the world. "And God said, Behold, I have given you every herb bearing seed, which is upon the face of all the earth, and every tree, in the which is the fruit of a tree yielding seed; to you, it shall be for meat. And to every beast of the earth, and every fowl of the air, and to everything that creepeth upon the earth, wherein there is life, I have given every green herb for meat: and it was so." (Genesis 1:29-30). At creation, God specified what man's diet should be. What do you think was the reason God didn't allow a man to choose their diet? I would imagine that the manufacturer of a car would know best how to look after that car. Should God not also know how best to look after His creation?

The subject of appetite is often taken very lightly even in the Christian world. Some argue that it's not a matter of salvation, as if forgetting that it was the very point on which our parents Adam and Eve failed. "And when the woman saw that the tree was good for food and that it was pleasant to the eyes, and a tree to be desired to make one wise, she took off the fruit thereof, and did eat, and gave also unto her husband with her, and he did eat." (Genesis 3:6).

Before I joined the military, I tasted alcohol a few times and had one puff of a cigarette. Back then I believed I was just experimenting, not knowing that I was opening the door to the life I ran away from while living at my dad's house. During my time in the military, I was introduced to a life of parties and drinking. Going to the clubs became a regular pastime. What happened during basic training whilst on a trip to France with fellow recruits, should have been an eye-opener for me, but it wasn't, I remembered that we went into a pub and at this point, I was new to drinking, so much that I always bought the same beer and only one or two maximum. It so happened that this pub didn't have the beer I wanted, so the barmaid suggested that I have a whisky instead. After one or two glasses of it, I found myself in the toilet hugging it for what felt like an eternity. The whole world was spinning and everything was blurry. Raising from distress to despair, I frantically searched the pub for my fellow recruits and they were nowhere to be found.

Alone in a strange country not knowing how to speak the language, I staggered outside to see if they were there, with no familiar face in sight. It started to dawn on me that I made a big mistake, and to make matters worse I couldn't even remember the name of the hotel we were staying at. However, God knows how to give us hope in our time of hopelessness, and the thought suddenly came to my mind to look for groups of people and follow them. I did it and went into another pub on the same street and they were there. Only a few people realized that I was missing. Their mind was just as numb as mine. After that experience, I promised myself that I will never get drunk again, but human promises are weak, because I got drunk many more times after that experience even when I had no intention of doing it. I was in an environment where everyone else was drinking or smoking and I ended up doing the same. What I was beholding, I was becoming.

"Our first duty toward God and our fellow beings is that of self-development. Every faculty with which the Creator has endowed us should be cultivated to the highest degree of perfection, so that we may be able to do the greatest amount of good of which we are capable. Hence that time is spent on a good account which is used in the establishment and preservation of physical and mental health. We cannot afford to dwarf or cripple any function of body or mind. As surely as we do this, we must suffer the consequences." (CD 15-CD 15.2). The consequences of that life I was living are still being painfully felt now and some of them will remain for the rest of my life. When we are young we see that kind of life as attractive; we tell ourselves that it is not so bad, but Satan works in subtle ways to deceive us.

We may not believe that diet is a salvational issue but it always has been. If God speaks about it in His word, then it's a matter of salvation. Diet has always been a test for God's people. "Then said the Lord unto Moses, Behold, I will rain bread from heaven for you; and the people shall go out and gather at a certain rate every day, that I may prove them, whether they will walk in my law, or no." (Exodus 16:4). Daniel and his friends recognized that eating the Babylonian's diet was a means of defiling themselves both spiritually, a numbing of the intellect which leads to debased morality, and physically as the wrong diet leads to bad health.

Many argue that eating meat is not a sin, because God commanded us to eat meat as if ignorant of the fact that God made it very clear that it was to shorten the life of mankind, because of our wickedness. Meat eating was not God's original plan as we have seen in Genesis 1:29-30, this command was given after the flood when the vegetation was destroyed. Meat eating was supposed to be temporary until the vegetation returned. Because we chose to make it permanently part of our diet, the lifespan of humans was significantly reduced after we became carnivores.

It is important for us to understand here that, just as the mixed multitudes during the Exodus wanted meat instead of manner; God allowed them to have what they wanted. However, this doesn't mean that God agreed with their request, because we know that they got sick and died as a result. Same is the case for Noah and his family after the flood in the sense that God allowed them to eat meat temporarily, the difference in this case is that, it was after the flood and the vegetation was destroyed. In both cases

God showed that; He understood our needs, He gives us freedom of choice and He knows what is best for us.

A physician understands the relation between diseases and the blood, so when symptoms can't be diagnosed by observation, they will recommend a blood test. Why? If there's an illness in the body the blood will be affected. The Bible doesn't hide this fact when it tells us that life is in the blood. "But that we write unto them, that they abstain from pollutions of idols, and fornication, and from things strangled, and from blood." (Acts 15:20). "But flesh with the life thereof, which is the blood thereof, shall ye not eat." (Genesis 9:4). "It shall be a perpetual statute for your generations throughout all your dwellings, that ye eat neither fat nor blood." (Leviticus 3:17).

"Moreover ye shall eat no manner of blood, whether it be of fowl or beast, in any of your dwellings." (Leviticus 7:26). "For it is the life of all flesh; the blood of it is for the life thereof: therefore I said unto the children of Israel, Ye shall eat the blood of no manner of flesh: for the life of all flesh is the blood thereof: whosoever eateth it shall be cut off." (Leviticus 17:14).

Some will argue at this point that they only eat kosher meat that has all the blood taken out, but this is not true as all the blood can't be taken out. The other aspect that is overlooked is that the fat must not be eaten also. It is a relatively new discovery in the scientific community that diseases are stored in fat. "To have good health, we must have good blood; for the blood is the current of life. It repairs waste and nourishes the body. When supplied with the proper food elements and when cleansed and vitalized by contact with pure air, it carries life and vigor to every part of the system. The more perfect the circulation, the better will this work be accomplished." (The Ministry of Healing, 271, 1905. CD 91.3).

"His course then tends downward; he is disobedient to the law of God and the laws of health. Appetite conquers him; inclination carries him away. It is easier for him to allow the powers of evil, which are always active, to drag him backward than to struggle against them and go forward. Dissipation, disease, and death follow. This is the history of many lives that might have been useful in the cause of God and humanity." ([Christian Temperance and Bible Hygiene, 41, 42] Counsels on Health, 107, 108, 1890. CD 15.4.)

"A failure to care for the living machinery is an insult to the Creator. There are divinely appointed rules which if observed will keep human beings from disease and premature death." (Letter 120, 1901). "One reason why we do not enjoy more of the blessing of the Lord is, we do not heed the light which He has been pleased to give us in regard to the laws of life and health." (The Review and Herald, May 8, 1883).

"God is as truly the author of physical laws as He is the author of the moral law. His law is written with His finger upon every nerve, every muscle, every faculty, which has been entrusted to man." (Christ's Object Lessons, 347, 348, 1900. CD 16.4-CD 17.1).

"It is as truly a sin to violate the laws of our being as it is to break the ten commandments. To do either is to break God's laws. Those who transgress the law of God in their physical organism will be inclined to violate the law of God spoken from Sinai." (CD 17.4).

"Through a perverted appetite, its organs and powers have become enfeebled, diseased, and crippled. And these results which Satan has brought about by his specious temptations, he uses to taunt God with. He presents before God the human body that Christ has purchased as His property; and what an unsightly representation of his Maker man is! Because man has sinned against his body, and has corrupted his ways, God is dishonored." (CD 18.4).

"Many have expected that God would keep them from sickness merely because they have asked Him to do so. But God did not regard their prayers, because their faith was not made perfect by works. God will not work a miracle to keep those from sickness who have no care for themselves but are continually violating the laws of health, and make no efforts to prevent disease. When we do all we can on our part to have health, then may we expect that the blessed results will follow, and we can ask God in faith to bless our efforts for the preservation of health.

He will then answer our prayer if His name can be glorified thereby. But let all understand that they have work to do. God will not work miraculously to preserve the health of persons who are taking a sure course to make themselves sick, by their careless inattention to the laws of health. Those who will gratify their appetite, and then suffer because of their intemperance, and take drugs to relieve them, may be assured that God will not interpose to save health and life which is so recklessly periled.

The cause has produced the effect. Many, as their last resort, follow the directions in the word of God and request the prayers of the elders of the church for their restoration to health. God does not see fit to answer prayers offered on behalf of such, for He knows that if they should be restored to health, they would again sacrifice it upon the altar of unhealthy appetite." (Spiritual Gifts 4a:144, 145, 1864. CD 26.1-CD 26.2).

"Let none who profess godliness regard with indifference the health of the body, and flatter themselves that intemperance is no sin, and will not affect their spirituality. A close sympathy exists between the physical and the moral nature." ([The Review and Herald, January 25, 1881] Counsels on Health, 67). "With our first parents, intemperate desire resulted in the loss of Eden. Temperance in all things has more to do with our restoration to Eden than men realize." (The Ministry of Healing, 129, 1905).

"Excessive indulgence in eating, drinking, sleeping, or seeing, is sin. The harmonious healthy action of all the powers of body and mind results in happiness; and the more elevated and refined the powers, the more pure and unalloyed the happiness." (Testimonies for the Church 4:417, 1880. CD 44.1).

"Self-indulgence debars the human agent from witnessing the truth. The gratitude we offer to God for His blessings is greatly affected by the food placed in the stomach. Indulgence of appetite is the cause of dissension, strife, discord, and many other evils. Impatient words are spoken and unkind deeds are done, dishonest practices are followed and passion is manifested, and all because the nerves of the brain are diseased by the abuse heaped upon the stomach." (Manuscript 93, 1901. CD 53.2-CD 53.3).

"In grains, fruits, vegetables, and nuts are to be found all the food elements that we need. If we will come to the Lord in the simplicity of mind, He will teach us how to prepare wholesome food free from the taint of flesh meat." (Manuscript 27, 1906. CD 92.2).

"Christ fought the battle upon the point of appetite, and came off victorious, and we also can conquer through strength derived from Him. Who will enter through the gates into the city? Not those who declare that they cannot break the force of appetite. Christ has resisted the power of him who would hold us in bondage; though weakened by His long fast of forty days, He withstood temptation and proved by this act that our cases are not hopeless. I know that we cannot obtain the victory alone; and how thankful we should be that we have a living Saviour, who is ready and willing to aid us! (Christian Temperance and Bible Hygiene, 19, 1890). "A pure and noble life, a life of victory over appetite and lust, is possible to everyone who will unite his weak, wavering human will to the omnipotent, unwavering will of God." (The Ministry of Healing, 176, 1905. CD 169-CD 170.1).

If we overcome our appetite then no other sin will be difficult for us to overcome. We are what we put inside of our bodies regardless of how it enters there, if it's not good for our health according to the word of God, then it is bad for it.

The change wasn't easy for me and at the same time not impossible, because I can see all the changes that God already made in me and many others that have been in a similar situation. We should never believe the lies that Satan tells us when we are at our weakest point, that we can't overcome, that we need it to relieve our stress, or that we are too sinful for God to forgive us. It's deception. God rescued me at my lowest and weakest point, regardless of how dark your world may seem, the God of light can pierce any darkness.

Chapter 9
Country Living

After many years of financial hardship and living from hand to mouth in England, failed business ventures, and odd jobs here and there, things started to get back on track; or so it seemed at the time. After the financial crash of 2008-2010, I was hanging on by a thread. After many Zero hours contracts, where no work hours were guaranteed, I found a full-time job and started to make ends meet again.

Thanks to God. Now I could put away some money for a holiday after paying the bills. I started to get comfortable with my situation, yet I could smell the pungent smell of weed coming into my bedroom window and could hear the worldly music until the ridiculous hours of the morning. Where I lived the houses were joined to each other. "Few realize the importance of shunning, so far as possible, all associations unfriendly to religious life. In choosing their surroundings, few make their spiritual prosperity the first consideration." (CL 5.1).

"Although everything God had made was in the perfection of beauty, and there seemed nothing wanting upon the earth which God had created to make Adam and Eve happy, yet He manifested His great love to them by planting a garden, especially for them. A portion of their time was to be occupied in the happy employment of dressing the garden, and a portion in receiving the visits of angels, listening to their instruction, and in happy meditation. Their labor was not wearisome, but pleasant and invigorating. This beautiful garden was to be their home, their special residence." (3SG 34 [1864]).

"What were the conditions chosen by the infinite Father for His Son? Secluded home in the Galilean hills; a household sustained by honest, self-respecting labor; a life of simplicity; daily conflict with difficulty and hardship; self-sacrifice, economy, and patient, gladsome service; the hour of study at His mother's side, with the open scroll of Scripture; the quiet of dawn or twilight in the green valley; the holy ministries of nature; the study of creation and providence; and the soul's communion with God--these were the conditions and opportunities of the early life of Jesus." (MH 365, 366 [1905]).

My surroundings were far from God's ideal, yet I started to become comfortable. Then the pandemic came and swept the rug from under my feet. As I kept up to date with current affairs, restriction after restriction were implemented in the country and at my Job. I started to realize that it was only a matter of time before it would affect me. Soon I was not able to enter the shopping mall in my town without a green pass and big supermarket shelves were emptied of 'essential items' and the waiting line stretched across the car park. It started to dawn on me how easy it was for things to change overnight when I went to my local shop to buy my usual three loaves of bread and could only get half for the price I paid for one previously.

Then one day I was told that for me to keep my job, I needed to do the PCR test. It was at this point I decided to look into the covid mandate, the testing kit, and the vaccines. After researching I concluded that it wasn't wise for me to take the test or take any of the vaccines. I saw ethical issues regarding the fluid in which the test samples cells are kept alive during transport, and that was enough for me to reject the test although there were other issues around my freedom of conscience. Furthermore, I don't take medication on a bad day and then I find myself being told that I am sick when there is nothing wrong with me.

It was very strange to see people who I knew for many years, social distance, because they believed that everyone might have covid. Talking about behavioral modification. I was working in health care at the time and although I could see that something was going around, I caught the covid symptoms as well, but instead of using the vaccine, I treated myself with natural remedies, exercise, and prayers. Within four days I was better. I understand that wasn't the case for many who died as a result of covid and I sympathized with their families.

I resigned from my job as I was given the ultimatum to do the test or leave. Now I was in a lockdown and had to go back to my old job where the restrictions were not in effect yet. Now I had more time to go over the scriptures to see if I had missed anything. By the easing of the restrictions in 2020, God has already convicted me about moving to do country living. It is thought provoking how I knew about country life for many years and was thinking of doing it sometime in the future when it was a convenient time. Then the pandemic made me realize that the convenient time was before covid came when I was spending my money going on holidays instead of making the preparations that God told me and all His people to make long before covid.

"Get out of the cities as soon as possible and purchase a little piece of land where you can have a garden, where your children can watch the flowers growing and learn from them lessons of simplicity and purity. (2SM 356 [1903]). "Let all who would understand the meaning of these things read the eleventh chapter of Revelation. Read every verse, and learn the things that are yet to take place in the cities. Read also the scenes portrayed in the eighteenth chapter of the same book." (MR 1518 [May 10, 1906]).

My wife and I started to research and plan our move to the countryside, we prayed and studied the information that God gave us in the bible and the writings of the prophetess Ellen Gould White, specifically the book's country living and last day events. We made a prayer list and went to God over and over again about what was on the list. So when the easing of the restrictions came, we already knew where we wanted to move to and were ready to move. Before the beginning of the second wave of covid lockdowns, we were crossing the border into Romania, looking at a great rainbow in the sky just after we crossed the border. I was reminded of God's rainbow of promises after the flood and then the flood of trials that I came out of, seemed far behind me. It was a new start and I saw the hands of God directing my journey and I rest assured in His arms.

This move to Romania wasn't the first time we went there as my wife is Romanian and we visited many places in the country before and were searching for property online. But now that we were asked to come and stay with my wife's sister-in-law and her husband while we look for somewhere to live, my wife was happy to make the move at that particular time before finding a house, I was reluctant, but I could see God working out a way for us to make the move exactly in the time when the Covid restrictions eased.

After choosing the parts of the country we wanted to live, armed with our list of many properties we found online and many prayers we started our search. Our budget wasn't very big because we were focusing on putting money away for holidays instead of God's plan. However, we knew that with the money we had, we needed to search for one to three hectares of land.

We searched and searched and searched even more and were disappointed over and over again, why? Because we came to learn that what people advertise online is usually exaggerated to rope in potential buyers. Viewings after viewings I saw my wife getting more and more discouraged. I was starting to feel that way, but I was sure that God was leading us and we must continue to search with determination.

Eventually, we went to view a property we found online and even though it needed a lot of work to make it liveable, it was the only property that we both felt was the right one. However, the paperwork needed to be done which was going to take about three more months. So we put in an offer, prayed about it and continued our search.

We went to view numerous properties after with the same feeling of disappointment, then one day the father of all the discouragement came and broke our backs. We found a house online that seemed to be exactly what we wanted in Mehedinți County and decided to make the twelve hours return drive to see the property, on our way we were communicating with the owner up until the final time we spoke with him to let him know that we are now in the country, and needed directions on how to get to the property. He then told us very coldly that he sold the property and we shouldn't bother coming. That day I could not hold back my disappointment, my wife was close to tears, if she didn't cry. I turned the car around and said that's it, I am not going to look for any more houses.

Sometimes we get so caught up in finding exactly what we want, that we fail to see what God has already provided for us. The house that we live in now is the only house we both agreed was what we planned to buy, as it fits most of the criteria that were on the list. But instead of ending our search there, waiting for the paperwork to be completed and waiting for God to open the way for us to buy that house, we went looking again up and down the country, meeting one disappointment after another.

God has already told us in His word that we are to leave the cities and told us why we should. Isn't it also His way to provide a place for us? "There are reasons why we should not build in the cities. In these cities, God's judgments are soon to fall." (Letter 158, 1902. CL 8.2). "The time is near when large cities will be swept away, and all should be warned of these coming judgments." (Evangelism, 29 (1910). CL 8.3).

Many may argue that God doesn't want everyone to leave the city, who will do the evangelism work in the city if all of God's people leave the city? they asked; "As God's commandment-keeping people we must leave the cities. As did Enoch, we must work in the cities but not dwell in them." (Ev 77, 78 [1899]). "The cities are to be worked from outposts. Said the messenger of God," "Shall not the cities be warned? Yes, not by God's people living in them but by visiting them, to warn them of what is coming upon the earth." (2SM 358).

"Do not consider it a privation when you are called to leave the cities and move out into the country places. There await rich blessings for those who will grasp them. By beholding the scenes of nature, the works of the Creator, by studying God's handiwork, imperceptibly you will be changed into the same image." (2SM 355, 356). "There is not one family in a hundred who will be improved physically, mentally, or spiritually, by residing in the city. Faith, hope, love, and happiness, can far better be gained in retired places, where there are fields and hills and trees. Take your children away from the sights and sounds of the city, away from the rattle and din of streetcars and teams, and their minds will become more healthy. It will be found easier to bring home to their hearts the truth of the Word of God." (AH 137).

If I was to tell you all what God has done for me since I started country living, I would have to write another book. He has blessed me in so many ways that I never considered. I have seen how He has put kindness in the hearts of the Romanian people to help us in many ways. My only regret now is that I didn't make the move sooner, because God has blessed us so much in a short space of time. I can imagine how much more He would have done if I had acted on His word sooner.

I would like all to understand that country living is hard work with great rewards, but it requires much faith, patience, and prayers. No one who loves city life will be at home in the country. I have seen people run back to city life within a year of living in the countryside. When God calls us to leave the city to live a life in rural areas, He is calling us to a life of character development, which is not without trials. We should not shun hardship, when we have to face it in our lives, God doesn't give us more than what we can overcome. These trials are what increase our faith and develop our character.

Since I started country living I have been in many situations where I was helpless in changing what was happening. In those times I truly learned how to just pray to God for help and leave everything to Him. Only now on my journey with God, I realized how God is powerful. I have seen Him change my seemingly impossible situations before my eyes and what is amazing is that even the people who made my situation impossible to overcome, God made it so they were the very one He used to do what needed to be done. I even heard them saying that they should not help me, but something tells them that they should. God is amazing and I pray that all of God's people make all the necessary preparations with the utmost urgency.

The history of this world is coming to its end and a great crisis is about to shake us all into chaos and hardship, the likes of which have never been seen or heard.

No one should believe that moving to rural areas alone will save us in this time, because it will not. Unless we are converted we will find country living to be a burden rather than joy, peace and character development, but God says to all His professed people; get out from the cities and that is my message to all. Life in rural areas will help us to develop the character we need when the crisis comes. It will also put us in a better position to grow provisions for ourselves and others when food and money will become scarce.

However, the best preparation that we can make now is to study our Bible, be in a constant attitude of prayer, and do the work of an Evangelist. Jesus preached many sermons but lives were changed by the life He lived. We need to meditate daily upon His life and live it. In doing so we will be true stewards of the heavenly kingdom.

Chapter 10

The Lord Delivered Me

God takes us to our extremes, so that we may know our limitations and that we may behold His glory and power. He has to take us to our extremities, so that all our self-dependencies may be removed. Just as gold is purified at extreme temperatures, so are we purified with extreme trials. Don't be overwhelmed and overcome by your trials, face them, overcome them. God is making a new you.

Deliverance came to me at the lowest point of my life. I was not looking for it. Certainly not. At that point in my life, death seemed as if it would be a welcome relief to all my pain and suffering. I was now coming to the end of my prodigal life before I started going back to church. I smoked and drank myself to nothing, the rent in arrears, the cold house, and an eviction notice hanging over my head. To make this worse, I was at the end of a five-year relationship that ended because of my lack of finances. To say that I was feeling low would be an understatement. The feeling was as if all my manhood was taken away and there was nothing left to live for. I felt as if I had failed to provide a proper home environment for my son and soon, we were going to be evicted.

Still smoking and drinking I couldn't see a way out. So I called on God to help me. What happened after still amazes me. I remember that day when I cried out to God for help, I was standing in the kitchen of the house I was about to be evicted from, and with tears running down my eyes I said Lord please help me, because I don't know what to do anymore. I was at my last, I was broken emotionally and physically.

It was then I heard that voice I can't forget, a wonderful fatherly voice that is full of care and compassion. He said to me anoint your head and your feet then stand up strong. I reacted instantly and reached for the bottle with olive oil and did exactly what I was told. As soon as I did it, until this day I am amazed. It was as if I was hit with a bolt of lightning and electric currents flowing throughout my body. It was so powerful that I had to close my hands into a fist and squeeze them like never before. I was doing it as if I was in excruciating pain, but I wasn't, the power that was flowing through my body wasn't pain, the best way I can describe it is overwhelming joy. I felt an unexplainable power and strength enter my body.

My heart felt so full at that moment as if it was about to explode and I clench my fist harder to be strong. It was such a beautiful and overwhelming feeling. Then time itself seemed to have stopped and then that voice spoke to me in words so clearly and simply, that I couldn't have any doubt or questions about what was happening, regardless of how amazing I thought everything was; saying; you will go many places and do many things in my name, you will be placed before leaders and rulers, but remember whatever is not of me, do not accept it, sweep it under the carpet.

As a Jamaican, I understood the phrase sweep it under the carpet very well, because it's a popular phrase in Jamaica. I understood it to mean that I must reject everything that is not of God and don't compromise in any way. I came to experience this when I was tested on working on the Sabbath in both of my previous employment.

Then I saw myself sitting in a dark room at a table with a candle lit on it. The light from the candle only shines around me and the rest of the room was very dark. My attention was then drawn to a large number of people inside the dark trying to get to me with so much anger, but it seemed as if the light was a natural barrier that was preventing them from getting to me. I thought in my mind why am I alone in this situation and why are these people so angry at me as if they wanted to kill me? Then I heard that voice again saying to me, you are not alone, I am with you.

After this, my experience finished and I felt such a perfect peace that I never felt before. It was as if the weight of the entire world was removed from my shoulders. To say that I was shocked and humbled by what happened would be an understatement, I was shocked that it happened to me. A big sinner such as myself. I spent weeks or months thinking about what happened and what anyone would say if I told them. Then one day I decided to make a video giving this testimony and posted it on my social media page.

"The Lord is not slack concerning his promise, as some men count slackness; but is long-suffering to us-ward, not willing that any should perish, but that all should come to repentance. But the day of the Lord will come as a thief in the night; in the which, the heavens shall pass away with a great noise, and the elements shall melt with fervent heat, the earth also and the works that are therein shall be burned up. Seeing then that all these things shall be dissolved, what manner of persons ought ye to be in all holy conversation and godliness." (2 Peter 3:9-11).

While I was in my miserable state I thought I had no hope left, I was led to believe that I was at the end of the road. However, God came and showed me that there's hope and in fact, my journey was just beginning. I don't deserve the immense love that God has for me. He loves us all and wants to deliver us from our lowest state.

"Now, belt your garment around your waist and arise, and speak to them all that I command you. Do not be dismayed before them, or I will make you dismayed before them. Now behold, I have made you today like a fortified city and like a pillar of iron and walls of bronze against the whole land, to the kings of Judah, to its leaders, to its priests, and the people of the land. And they will fight against you but they will not overcome you, for I am with you to save you, declares the Lord." (Jeremiah 1:17-19).

When God rescues us, He fixes our broken state and makes us rescuers. He has great work for everyone who will come to Him. He is a mighty God that can save anyone who chooses to be saved, whatever your lowest state is, He can come and rescue you. Just call out to Him, Lord! Please help me.

"The Lord is my rock, and my fortress, and my deliverer; my God, my strength, in whom I will trust; my buckler, and the horn of my salvation, and my high tower." (Psalm 18:2).

I know now what God can do for me and I know also that; Satan the enemy would have killed me if he could. It's full-time now that we understand that we are at war and the enemy is working tirelessly to destroy us. We have a work to warn others of the enemy and his snares. Yes, we will have opposition, but remember you are not alone. God is with you.

"As the people of God approach the perils of the last days, Satan holds earnest consultation with his angels as to the most successful plan of overthrowing their faith. He sees that the popular churches are already lulled to sleep by his deceptive power. By pleasing sophistry and lying wonders, he can continue to hold them under his control. Therefore he directs his angels to lay their snares, especially for those who are looking for the second advent of Christ and endeavoring to keep all the commandments of God." (TM 472.1).

Satan says to his angels; "We must cause distraction and division. We must destroy their anxiety for their souls, and lead them to criticize, judge, accuse and condemn one another, and to cherish selfishness and enmity. For these sins, God banished us from His presence; and all who follow our example will meet a similar fate." (TM 475.2).

Our Lord and Saviour Jesus Christ are calling us to come to His fold, and allow Him to rescue us. When you are rescued, go and tell others what Satan is doing. Expose this imposter, so that others can be rescued, and let's meet on the heavenly shores. Don't be afraid to stand for Jesus in defiance of the enemy.

Chapter 11

Holding Back The Tears

For 6,000 years sin has been wreaking havoc upon humanity. What is sin? Is there a reason for it? Can it be overcome in this life? How can it be overcome? Will there ever be a world without sin? The Bible teaches that sin is the breaking of God's Ten Commandments. No reason is given for sin. Why should there be any reason given? The Bible tells that Lucifer was the highest exalted among the angels, he was a covering cherub that stood next to the throne of God. Instead of protecting the laws of God, he started to rebel against them. He was created perfect and was lacking in nothing. But the created wanted to covet the place of his Creator.

"The fall of man filled all heaven with sorrow. The world that God had made was blighted with the curse of sin and inhabited by beings doomed to misery and death. There appeared no escape for those who had transgressed the law. Angels ceased their songs of praise. Throughout the heavenly courts, there was mourning for the ruin that sin had wrought." (PP 63.1).

"The Son of God, heaven's glorious Commander, was touched with pity for the fallen race. His heart was moved with infinite compassion as the woes of the lost world rose before Him. But divine love had conceived a plan whereby man might be redeemed. The broken law of God demanded the life of the sinner. In all the universe there was but one who could, on behalf of man, satisfy its claims. Since the divine law is as sacred as God Himself, only one equal with God could make atonement for its transgression. None but Christ could redeem fallen man from the curse of the law and bring him again into harmony with Heaven. Christ would take upon Himself the guilt and shame of sin—sin so offensive to a holy God that it must separate the Father and His Son. Christ would reach to the depths of misery to rescue the ruined race." (PP 63.2).

It is important in laying out the delicate subject of sin and its effects, that I begin with the good news first. We are told that as soon as mankind fell into sin, Jesus came forth to be our Savior. So we are not alone in this, God has not abandoned us. There's hope in our Lord and Saviour Jesus Christ.

The majority of the Christian world believes that they will be sinning until Jesus returns, so therefore, it's not possible to overcome sin in this life. The rationale for this kind of thinking lies in the false teaching that we have a sinful nature that can't be changed until Jesus comes and makes us righteous.

The problem with this gospel is that it leads people to state unpreparedness, it deceives them into believing that no change is required in life, when they come to God. So instead of becoming Christians, they end up just being church members.

Christ has given us the greatest example of how to overcome a life of sin, and this can be seen clearly in the way He lived His life on this earth. We can also overcome this world by following His examples. But if we don't believe that He has the power to forgive and cleanse us from our sins, then we will not be able to overcome them.

"There hath no temptation taken you but such as is common to man: but God is faithful, who will not suffer you to be tempted above that ye are able; but will with the temptation also make a way to escape, that ye may be able to bear it." (1 Corinthians 10:13).

In a world so filled with death and despair, people are now looking for a way out. Many desperate souls are with their eyes looking in the heavens wondering, is there a God up there, can He save me? They look to different religions and find confusion there, then they look to the examples of celebrities and religious leaders and are let down. Is there any hope?

As my son's dog lay dying he looked at me holding back the tears, as if trying to be strong, looking at me he said; "daddy isn't there anything we can do?" I said to him, my son there's isn't anything we can do now, the dog is taking its last breath. The feeling of sadness and helplessness came over me, so familiar was that feeling, because I watched my dog die when I was about the same age as my son.

This pain and sadness don't stop at the experience of watching your pet suffering from the dark hold of death. When your loved one dies the cold knife of sadness pierces the heart deeper, especially when we know that the individual didn't have any relationship with God. Death in any situation is a horrible experience for anyone affected by it. I have seen enough death already to know.

The news of my dad's death was no exception. It was even worse for the fact that I had just sent off my passport and paperwork to the home office to apply for my citizenship and couldn't afford to withdraw the application or even the flight to Jamaica. I was disappointed that I could not go, but not for anything else, because the God I serve can also do miraculous things ahead of time. He knows the future and He has proven it to me many times.

After I left my dad's house to live with my mom. I saw less and less of him until decades passed without me seeing him. We were not close as I wished we were, and after many years of living in England, I was given a resident visa and could now travel. I went to Jamaica to visit him with the hope that we could work on our relationship. Things didn't go as planned, because I realized that my dad had not changed in all the years I didn't see him. I left my dad's house after an argument with the intention of not going back to see him again.

My dad was always the person who just didn't give me any chance to express myself or give my opinion, he was always a talker and not a listener. So whatever issue I was facing, I knew that I could not talk to him about it. He was just really bad at being a father. But somehow he manages occasionally to let us know that he loves all of his children. The trouble was that I could not see or feel it.

None of this can be said of my Lord and Saviour Jesus Christ, I don't need to tell Him what I am going through or wonder if He loves or cares for me, because He makes it very clear in all what He has done for me.

During my kitchen experience, Jesus spoke to me in words clear as day and said, call all your family and fix any problems you have with them. The first person that came to my mind was my dad. I felt such an overwhelming push to call him and tell him exactly how I felt, but resisted for maybe a day and a half or more. I just kept thinking that he never listened to what I had to say, and whenever I said anything about how he treated and spoke to me when he was drunk, he would never accept anything that I was saying, instead, he would curse me. So I had no interest in speaking with him, but the Lord kept impressing my heart to speak with him. I remember that day I could not sleep and was thinking of calling him until about 4 am when I finally did.

When I think about what happened after my dad picked up the phone, I have absolutely no doubt that it was a miracle. It was as if I was speaking to someone else, certainly not my dad. I started talking with him by saying hello dad, how are you? I want to talk with you and I hope that you will take the time to listen. His answer was; "ok son I am listening," I told him how I felt about our argument that we had, and he listened, explained, and apologized. You must understand, my dad was always right according to him, and apologizing was very rare.

I then asked him why he wasn't a good father to me. Questions like this would erupt into him cursing me to scorn, but not this time, voice filled with unseen gentleness and compassion, as if sent of heaven, said; "my son, I ran away from home when I was 12 years of age, because my parents treated me very bad and beaten me very badly whenever he was rude, I don't know how to be a good father, because I didn't have one and I grew up on the street going from house to house.

Suddenly everything made absolute sense, growing up I heard him saying so many times that he ran away from home when he was 12 years old, but being a typical child, paid no attention to what he was saying. Now after running away from home myself and becoming a father as well, seeing how unprepared I was when I found out I was going to be a dad, everything made sense to me. I also didn't know how to be a good father because, growing up I didn't have any example of what that is supposed to look like, so only then I came to the realization.

Running away from home at the age of 12 meant that my dad didn't get the education I did, to read books on parenting and most of all, he didn't study the Bible to get the true example of how a father should be. Everything made sense now and that early morning I felt the weight of many years lifted from my shoulders. I was even able to tell my dad that I was a Christian now, he said that he was very happy for me and he also changed his life and is talking with God.

I am very sure that if I didn't listen to God and speak to my dad that early morning, I would not receive the peace with him that I longed for so many years. After my conversation with dad, I called two of my sisters, because I knew that they must have had similar questions as I did, to tell them that God told me to call and speak with dad and I did, I told them to talk with him about whatever you want to talk to him about, he will listen. They thought I was going mad. Two weeks after I received the news that he died from bowel cancer. I didn't even know that he was sick. One of my sisters called me in tears after she heard the news asking me how I knew that dad was sick and dying and didn't tell her. I didn't know, but God did and He gave us all the warnings we needed ahead of time.

God has also told us ahead of time that one day he will rid the world of sin and death, and there will be a world where there is no more pain and suffering. I don't know what my dad spoke to Jesus about or if I will ever see him again. What I know is that I want to be in heaven and I wish to see all my family and friends there, even you, my dearest reader. I have this hope, because I know that there is a righteous judge in heaven. Who is also our intercessor? But remember heaven is for all who have overcome by the blood of the Lamb that takes away the sins of the world.

In just a little while longer if we are faithful we will be able to walk and talk with our creator. Soon all our questions will be answered and all our trials, pain and suffering will be taken away. God records all our tears and will heal us entirely.

Chapter 12

Jesus is coming! Jesus is coming! Jesus is Coming!

A s I lay in a field with other people, the place I was in seemed to be a camp of some sort in the mountains, because people were camping in tents and caravans also; I was awakened by an indescribable force of the wind. Tents were swept into the air and carried away, caravans were on their sides, then I noticed that I could see the effects of the wind, but could not feel its impact.

I called out with a loud voice to the people, but their supernatural panic and fright were too much for them to notice me. Because the camp was on the slope of a hill, in an area that was flat enough, very similar to where I am now, but without any buildings, we were camping further down the slope away from the road, closer to the trees. I started frantically to run around, trying to get everyone's attention. It was as if I had been pulled to the top of the hill.

I ran to anyone I could find on my way to the road at the top of the hill. As I got there I realized that not everyone came with me to the top of the hill. My heart was filled with sadness that was suddenly swept away by the sudden appearance of a small distant light in the sky, surrounded by dark clouds the size of a man's fist, the light was brilliant in its brightness. Never a star shines brighter, I recognize the light instantly and then another force of wind greater than the one that was, in comparison meaningless, coming from the direction of the light. The force of this wind coming from the heavens was so great that it became the only wind that was blowing.

With overwhelming joy I began to shout; Jesus is coming! Jesus is coming! Jesus is coming! I was shouting so much that I woke my wife and myself. Oh, what indescribable joy I felt standing on that hill and looking at my redeemer approaching the earth to claim His long-lost sheep.

Oh, I long for that day, the day when I hear the voice of my shepherd and see His face and behold his glory. The world is cold and dark enough and the winds of strife are ever before us. Is it not full-time now that we seek out our savior while He can still be found?

"God will accept nothing but purity and holiness; one spot, one wrinkle, one defect in the character, will forever debar the unrepentant sinner from heaven, with all its glories and treasures. Ample provisions have been made for all who sincerely, earnestly, and thoughtfully set about the work of perfecting holiness in the fear of God. Strength, grace, and glory have been provided through Christ, to be brought by ministering angels to the heirs of salvation. None are so low, so corrupt and vile, that they cannot find in Jesus, who died for them, strength, purity, and righteousness if they will put away their sins, cease their course of iniquity, and turn with full purpose of heart to the living God...I was referred to this scripture: "Let not sin therefore reign in your mortal body, that ye should obey it in the lusts thereof. Neither yield ye your members as instruments of unrighteousness unto sin: but yield yourselves unto God, as those that are alive from the dead, and your members as instruments of righteousness unto God." (Romans 6:12, 13." CH 568.1-CH 569.1).

"Not one of us will ever receive the seal of God while our characters have one spot or stain upon them. It is left with us to remedy the defects in our characters, to cleanse the soul temple of every defilement. Then the latter rain will fall upon us as the early rain fell upon the disciples on the day of Pentecost." (CET 189.2).

"Now when Jesus was born in Bethlehem of Judea in the days of Herod the king, behold, there came wise men from the East to Jerusalem, saying, Where is He that is born King of the Jews? for we have seen His star in the East, and are come to worship Him."

"The wise men from the East were philosophers. They belonged to a large and influential class that included men of noble birth and comprised much of the wealth and learning of their nation. Among these were many who imposed on the credulity of the people. Others were upright men who studied the indications of Providence in nature, and who were honored for their integrity and wisdom. Of this character were the wise men who came to Jesus.

The light of God is ever shining amid the darkness of heathenism. As these magi studied the starry heavens and sought to fathom the mystery hidden in their bright paths, they beheld the glory of the Creator. Seeking clearer knowledge, they turned to the Hebrew Scriptures. In their land were treasured prophetic writings that predicted the coming of a divine teacher. Balaam belonged to the magicians, though at one time a prophet of God; by the Holy Spirit he had foretold the prosperity of Israel and the appearance of the Messiah; and his prophecies had been handed down by tradition from century to century. But in the Old Testament, the Saviour's advent was more clearly revealed. The magi learned with joy that His coming was near and that the whole world was to be filled with the knowledge of the glory of the Lord.

The wise men had seen a mysterious light in the heavens upon that night when the glory of God flooded the hills of Bethlehem. As the light faded, a luminous star appeared and lingered in the sky. It was not a fixed star nor a planet, and the phenomenon excited the keenest interest. That star was a distant company of shining angels, but of this the wise men were ignorant. Yet they were impressed that the star was of special import to them. They consulted priests and philosophers and searched the scrolls of the ancient records. The prophecy of Balaam declared, "There shall come a Star out of Jacob, and a Scepter shall rise out of Israel." (Numbers 24:17). Could this strange star have been sent as a harbinger of the Promised One? The magi had welcomed the light of heaven-sent truth; now it was shed upon them in brighter rays. Through dreams, they were instructed to go in search of the newborn Prince." (DA 59.1-DA 60.1).

"They have reached the land of Israel, and are descending the Mount of Olives, with Jerusalem in sight, when, lo, the star that has guided them all the weary way rests above the temple, and after a season fades from their view. With eager steps they press onward, confidently expecting the Messiah's birth to be the joyful burden of every tongue. But their inquiries are in vain. Entering the holy city, they repair the temple. To their amazement, they find none who seem to know the newborn king. Their questions call forth no expressions of joy, but rather of surprise and fear, not unmingled with contempt.

The priests are rehearsing traditions. They extol their religion and their piety, while they denounce the Greeks and Romans as heathens, and sinners above others. The wise men are not idolaters, and in the sight of God they stand far higher than do these, His professed worshipers; yet they are looked upon by the Jews as heathen. Even among the appointed guardians of the Holy Oracles, their eager questioning touched no chord of sympathy." (DA 60.3-DA 61.1)

It is horrifying for me to find myself repeating the mistakes of our forefathers. While filled with pride the Scribes and Pharisees were passed by, instead of a state of watchfulness, the darkness of tradition cheered on by the deceiver was the driving force behind their religion. The coming Redeemer was a distant memory. Awakened by watchmen from the east, whom the Jews saw as gentiles, they began to worry about their image and positions.

Instead of greeting these wise men with happiness and joy, they were met with animosity. I have lost count of how many times the wise men of today are shunned and rejected as they open up the prophecies and show that Christ's second coming is even at the door, because their messages hit a particular sin and cut to our pride. We are living in a time when some of God's professed people are afraid to preach against popular sins, some are even afraid to say the word sin. So instead of hearing a message that will knock us to our senses, we are left with a watered-down message that is not fit for purpose.

However, as watchmen living at the close of this Earth's history, we are called to preach the three angels' messages. Like the wise men they should create a stir in our ranks and if heeded will bring change to our lives, prepare us for Christ's second coming and bring light to the world. The sad truth is that so many of us will allow unbelief to prevent us from entering the Kingdom of God.

"And I saw another angel fly amid heaven, having the everlasting gospel to preach unto them that dwell on the earth, and to every nation, and kindred, and tongue, and people, Saying with a loud voice, Fear God, and give glory to him; for the hour of his judgment is come: and worship him that made heaven, and earth, and the sea, and the fountains of waters. And there followed another angel, saying, Babylon is fallen, is fallen, that great city because she made all nations drink of the wine of the wrath of her fornication. And the third angel followed them, saying with a loud voice, If any man worships the beast and his image and receives his mark in his forehead, or his hand, The same shall drink of the wine of the wrath of God, which is poured out without mixture into the cup of his indignation; and he shall be tormented with fire and brimstone in the presence of the holy angels, and in the presence of the Lamb: And the smoke of their torment ascendeth up for ever and ever: and they have no rest day nor night, who worship the beast and his image, and whosoever receiveth the mark of his name. Here is the patience of the saints: here are they that keep the commandments of God, and the faith of Jesus." (Revelation 14:6 - 12).

As this message sounds louder and louder throughout the earth, people will become more aware of their true condition and see their need for our Lord and Saviour Jesus Christ. We must strive to be like Him. Let not our pride cause us to be passed by when sealing work is taking place on the earth. God has put the story of the three wise men as an example for us who are living at the end of time, so that we may not make the same mistakes. We can make it home, because God has done everything for us to do so, but we have our part to do also. Shall we not be laborers together with Christ? "I must work the works of Him that sent Me while it is day; the night cometh when no man can work." If all of God's professed people put away themselves and do the work He has called us to do, our Saviour would already have returned.

I take great comfort in knowing that God cannot lie, it's simply not part of His character. Whatever He says He will do, He will do it. In all my life He has kept His word, even when I didn't keep mine, He was still faithful to His. God wants to save me and has done everything for this to happen. He wants to save you also. "Greater love hath no man than this, that a man lay down his life for his friends." (John 15:13). He went to the extent of dying for us to show us how much He cares for us and the validity of His word. You can also take great comfort in His word when he says that He will come again. "Let not your heart be troubled: ye believe in God, believe also in me. In my Father's house are many mansions: if it were not so, I would have told you. I am going to prepare a place for you. And if I go and prepare a place for you, I will come again, and receive you unto myself; that where I am, there ye may be also." (John 14:1-3).

What a joy it will be for all the redeemed when Jesus returns to rescue all of His people. This is a once in a lifetime opportunity that I can say that I don't want to miss. I also encourage all of you my readers, do not miss it.

Bibliography

Works cited from these sources:

1. The Bible
The King James Bible 1611
New American Standard Bible 1971

2. Ellen G. White
Counsels on Diet and Foods (CD) (1938)
Country Living (CL) (1946)
Counsels on Health (CH) (1923)
Christian Experience and Teachings (CET) (1922)
Christ Object Lesson (COL) (1923)
Early Writings (EW) (1882)
Evangelism (EV) (1946)
Letter 120, (1901)
Manuscript Releases, vol.21 (MR1518) (May 10, 1906)
Patriarchs and Prophets (PP) (1890)
Selected Messages Book 2 (2SM) (1903)
Spiritual Gifts. Volume 3 (3SG) (1864)
Testimonies for the church volume five (5T) (1889)
Testimonies to ministers and gospel workers (TM) (1890-1898)
The Adventist Home (AH) (1952)
The Desire of Ages (DA) (1898)
The Ministry of Healing (MH) (1905)

The Review and Herald, May 8, (1883)

3.   **Motherjones.com**

4.   **Britanica.com**

About the author

Melbourne Charity Powell was born in 1984 in Mandeville, Jamaica. He lived there until he was 8 years of age then moved to Kingston 9, St. Andrew until he was 17 years when he moved to England. His first job in England was as a paperboy, then later at 18 years old he enlisted in the British Army. Some years later he was trained in the Health care sector where he worked until 2020.

Since 2016 he founded Your Truth Ministries and has been sharing the Gospel since. His love for sharing God's word keeps growing as He sees the results in His own life and of others. Melbourne has a son, Tyrone P. Powell who is now 13 years old and they have been residing in a rural part of Bihor, Romania since 2020.

Address: Vilcelele, Suplacu de Barcau
E-Mail: flatstone@hotmail.co.uk
Phone Number: 0765200396